1845–1870
AN UNTOLD STORY OF NORTHERN CALIFORNIA

The American Settler's First Documented
Accounts of their Unwelcome Arrival

A historical non-fiction narrative with
evidence based on personal journals, diaries,
news articles and essays, detailing the first hostile
pioneering experiences of Northern California.

Daniel L. Smith

Revealing Historical Truths Through
First-Hand Accounts

PO Box 221974 Anchorage, Alaska 99522-1974
books@publicationconsultants.com—www.publicationconsultants.com

ISBN Number: 978-1-59433-853-3
eBook ISBN Number: 978-1-59433-824-3

Library of Congress Catalog Card Number: 2019952138

Copyright 2019 Daniel L. Smith
—First Edition—

All rights reserved, including the right of reproduction in any form, or by any mechanical or electronic means including photocopying or recording, or by any information storage or retrieval system, in whole or in part in any form, and in any case not without the written permission of the author and publisher.

Manufactured in the United States of America

Dedication

These facts I write are dedicated to my entire family.

All of our past relatives have moved out to California at some point in time.

However your outlook on historical events, I hope you see the truth in these words.

... you all know who you are.

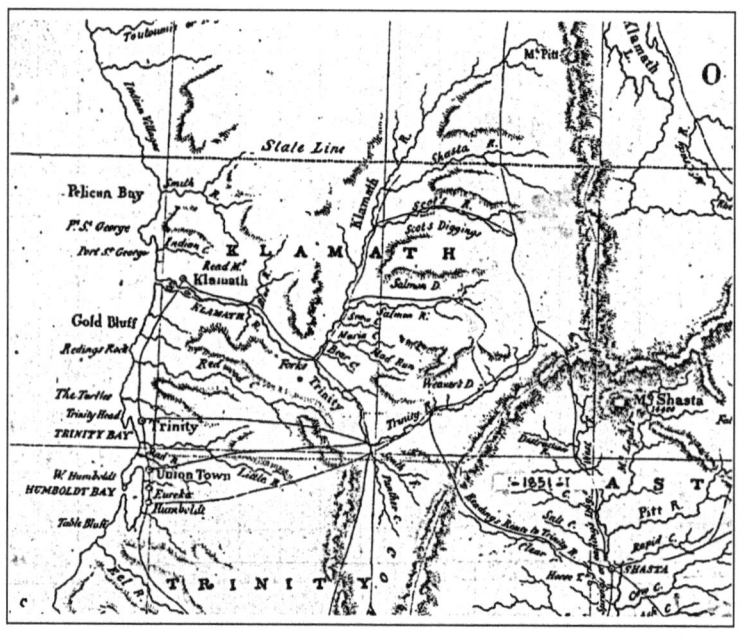

Northern California Area Reference Map

"In early May, 1846, Klamath Indians attacked an expedition under the command of Captain John Charles Fremont on the west shore of Upper Klamath Lake, just a few miles north of the California border. Fremont responded by sending out a retaliatory party under the leadership of Kit Carson...

This incident marked the opening of conflict..."

Loring White – Winning Essay in the Second Annual A.N.C.R.R. Contest in Local History, 1974

CONTENTS

FOREWORD	7
SPANISH INFLUENCE on CALIFORNIA	13
NEW AMERICAN SETTLERS	19
BAD APPLES	29
UNSTABLE CALIFORNIA	35
TRIBAL CUSTOMS & RELIGION	44
NATIVE JUSTICE	56
FAILURES OF RESTRAINT	65
THE GOVENOR & THE MILITIA	71
DEPREDATIONS	84
A SERIOUS INACCURACY	93
HOSTILITY IN UPPER CALIFORNIA	99
THE CONFLICT PEAKS	106
A BOIL OVER	114
CONCLUSION	119
BIBLIOGRAPHY	125

FOREWORD

I have lived all over the United States, and I mean that quite literally. I was born in New Hampshire and lived in nearly a dozen states, both East and West. However of all the places I have lived, I spent most of my time in California. Within the State, my experiences have taken me from the Northern to the Southern border. I have spent time in many different towns and cities, both urban and rural. The time spent in these towns and large cities were mostly attributed to professional interests.

Of course, that was a time past and it is because of these experiences in California that I can even talk about my understanding of Humboldt County by moving there in the first place. I moved into the City of Eureka, located in the County of Humboldt during the summer of 1995 from Washington State, and stayed there until the summer of 1998. My father would end up taking a promotion and a transfer of duty station immediately. He was a military man.

It was during the three years that I was living there that I noticed what I perceived as very heavy indigenous American bias being dumped into the counties educational system, as well as this same point-of-view gradually being pumped into the states larger cities. There seemed to be a purposeful excess of native cultural influence too. This looks okay from a local resident to northern California, but to an outsider looking in such as myself, it seemed to have created a synthetic thought process of displaced hate towards the American settlers culture.

I have found there to be a lot of misinformation and plenty of opinions available. There are sadly many disinformed and misled Americans with regard to the indigenous natives of Northern California. Personal experiences will vary of course. My own experiences opened my eyes to fallacy people hold in their minds. This all has led to a false understanding of what truths actually exist within the pseudo-relations and depredations of both the indigenous natives and the Americans from the east who settled in Northern California.

I seek to find what was truly to blame for the relational animosity that enabled non-stop multi-cultural conflict. 1845 to 1870 was chaotic. Famous author Mark Twain said it best, "Gold-rush California was a tumultuous place... a wild, free, disorderly, grotesque society!" The events that sparked the troubles between the American settlers and the natives is well documented in local historical records. It is seemingly harder and harder to dig up the information anymore in regards to native antagonization.

The good news however is that the truth is not at all lost or gone. I have been able to pull up resources

Daniel L. Smith

from many local, state, and national historical archives to research both, primary and secondary sources. This provides the reader with the most accurate information regarding truth in what had actually happened in the events that involved the American settlers and the natives of Northern California.

This information is all linked to factual legal documentation, most in original hand written form from the 19th century (excluding secondary sources). As I have spent countless hours and days, researching and investigating root causes of native and settler conflict; I have found that both cultures have three things in common that play a distinct role in their relationships. One, cultural influence. Two, physical evidence. Three, religious inseparability. It takes all three spheres to present fact in history.

As the 1800's would carry on, however, more and more peoples of Euro-American, Asian, South American, Kanaka (Hawaii natives of early California), and other ethnic groups actively underwrote Northern California's story. I believe that typical Americans forget that individuals who immigrated to the U.S. typically brought with them their own home cultures way of doing life as well.

Settler and native diplomatic conduits in trusting began to wane, as close relationships between individuals gradually became less and less mutually beneficial. Conflicts between the predominantly white settler community and local natives increased. Almost not even perceivable at first, but to an increasing degree after the year 1850. In this literature, I investigate and narrate the way showing the reader that not all local natives were not for necessarily supportive or even wanted coexistence, nor would the two societies meld together gracefully.

From the beginning the United States was made to deal with the question of Native Americans because of the violent hostility of the local tribes and the irresistible pressure on the native tribal lands in search of free property and material wealth. The Federal Indian policy in California at the time of settlement included making treaties with the tribes; in which they were granted the right to occupy certain geographical regions, and American settlers were absolutely prohibited from stepping foot into these said tribal areas.

By cooperation between the native tribes and U.S. government both worked together to establish trading houses, for example, among the tribes. Within them, they implemented some of the typical ways that the settlers practiced husbandry, ranching, and household arts. This would have amounted to a work-visa (cultural building) program we would see today. This was one method of making cultural adjustment between the indigenous natives and the American settlers.

In making the cultural adjustments with the local native tribes of the northern California region, the United States government was guided by the principles upon which civilized nations had for a long time based their treatment of uncivilized peoples. These principles were restated and reinforced by decisions of the Supreme Court, which, while recognizing the native tribes and further stated which formal treaties were to be made, regarded the governments of civilized states as having sovereignty over lands and peoples within their jurisdiction.[1]

To further state fact, there was no tribal organization as it existed on any other parts of the North American plate. The local native tribes of the northern California area were many in population. Even though they numbered many and had the same ethnic ties – each tribe was just a little unique in their cultural customs. However, the only actual real tie that held the native tribes together was language and topography of the land; more than any political or social ties.[2]

In the end, the United States must be credited with a fraction of sincerity in its efforts to relieve the hostile native dilemma plaguing the northern California settlers in the early years of its history. The following literature has been presented in a way that makes for fluid reading. This, more than focusing on the exact chronological event by date and time. Of course, as a historical non-fiction piece, the following narrative has been illustrated in a way that makes for easy reading. The events in this

---

1   Ellison, William H. "The Federal Indian Policy in California, 1846-1860." *The Mississippi Valley Historical Review* 9, no. 1 (1922), pp. 37-39. doi: 10.2307/1886099.
2   *Handbook of American Indians*, north of Mexico (Bureau of American ethnology, *Bulletin* no. 30, edited by Fredrick M. Hodge – Washington, 1907-1910), Hubert H. Bancroft, *Native races* (San Francisco, 1883), vols. 1, 3, 4.

chapter are transliterated in a way that is made easier to understand for every reader.

The truth is, I have accounted for over 400 different native depredations occurring against the settlers of Northern California on at least 90 pages of paper. Keeping in mind the amount of information available, it would be almost impossible to recount and transliterate all relevant sources. However, as best as possible only the most significant depredations will be briefly explained and narrated for better situational understanding.

SPANISH INFLUENCE ON CALIFORNIA

Northern California, is a scene of majestic redwood forests, beautiful rocky coastlines, and lush inner-landscapes that can only be imagined today. The land known to us today as Humboldt County, for example, had been called home to indigenous tribal peoples for some time prior to the arrival of Europeans.[3] In pristine Northern California, over a dozen tribes made up the encompassed swath of land from Klamath to the Eel River on the coast. This territory also ranged inland to include its city neighbors of Weaverville and Shasta. All local tribes of Northern California, like all civilizations, have cultural tendencies that are all based around religion, resources, customs and family (religion and family – which surprisingly many intellectuals tend to leave out of contemporary texts in terms of historical importance to events).[4]

---

3 Ziegler, Herbert, and Jerry Bentley. *Bentley, Traditions & Encounters: A Global Perspective on the Past*, 6th ed. New York, NY: McGraw-Hill, 2014. p. 34.
4 Smith, Daniel L. *Our America: Our Life & Our Culture*. Eureka, CA.: Independent, 2018. p. 48.

1845-1870 An Untold Story of Northern California

To understand California's beginnings is to understand that according to Europe and the rest of the non-indigenous world – California was a Spanish territory.[5] It was in 1587 that Conquistador Pedro de Unamumo was given orders on the Spanish monarchy to explore the coasts of California. At the time however, the Spanish crown believed that California was its own unique island.[6] Conquistador Unamumo would end up pulling into the area of Morro Bay where he led an armed landing party of 12 men, accompanied by a priest. When attempted contact was made, the landing party was showered on with arrows and spears. Five of the men were wounded – two were killed.[7]

On June 11th 1775, two Spanish Naval conquistadors, Bruno de Heceta and Juan Francisco de la Bodega y Quadra, landed on Trinity Head Point where they placed the Catholic cross and immediately his landing party was rained on by native arrows.[8] It was at this point Spanish officials ordered explorers not to leave the safety of their ships, or cargo. Colonizing Spaniards were in California for economic as well as political reasons, and religious purposes. It seems as though the Spanish explorers

---

5   Ellison, William H. "Indian Policy in California." 21, no. 1 (Fall), 2-3.
6   Sedler, Kathy. "History of Humboldt County, California." *Historic Record Co., Los Angeles*, 1915. Ch. 5, Para. 1.
7   Sedler, K. Ibid., Ch. 5, Para. 6.
8   Tovell, Freeman M. (2008). At the Far Reaches of Empire: The Life of Juan Francisco De La Bodega Y Quadra. University of British Columbia Press. pp. 22–23. ISBN 978-0-7748-1367-9.

however at the time were more out for the monarchy's intentions than their own person.

There was a lot of complicated quasi-relationships between the Spanish and the indigenous natives of California. Due to implemented policies by Spanish authority, the ultimate result of Spanish empiricism would be a general cultural oppression to the indigenous tribes of California. This oppression was the result of the Jesuit Catholic missions, including political officers appointed by Spain and their policies towards the indigenous natives of California.[9] These natives were not asked to convert, they were forced into the Catholic mission system.

Once on mission grounds, it became a cultural shock to the indigenous people who had the unfortunate chance of being pushed into this system. To get a better inside look at the reality of Spanish California missions is to understand their goals. It was to create temporary institutes to civilize the natives by giving them a proper education, as well as providing experience in European skillsets of labor, and knowledge of their political and social customs. The next phase of the process was 'gente du razon' or – a civilized people of mixed native and Spanish ethnicity. In the end, the Spanish would dissolve the missions after the natives were civilized, allowing the

---

9 Ellison, William H. "The Federal Indian Policy in California, 1846-1860." *The Mississippi Valley Historical Review* 9, no. 1 (1922): p. 33.

1845-1870 An Untold Story of Northern California

native converts to manage the mission lands. Further, the natives would become tax-paying Spanish citizens.[10]

The Spanish authorities would then secularize (remove the religious purposes of the institute) the lands the mission was on – ultimately forming a sort of vassal, but unincorporated part of Spanish-colonial society. The intended Spanish plan for the mission system would end up collapsing on itself. When the natives of the missions did not renounce their customs and traditions for strict Catholicism, they were punished with intensity. Anytime a native broke any religious, work, or fleshly rules laid out by the mission, Catholic authorities would administer punishment of even minor incident. [11]

Extra manual-labor, less food provisions… or worse: shackled in chains, whipped, and held in prison-like confinement. As time would inevitably move forward, the economic policies of the mission would etch out a permanent mark on the landscape of Northern California. Geographical change with the Catholic missions economic and their religious purposes would serve to negatively affect the early-settlers of Northern California starting in the mid-nineteenth century.[12] This particular event in history would show the threat of substantial

---

10 Olson-Raymer, Geyle. "The Discovery, Exploration, and Founding of Spanish California." HSU – Dept. of History. Last modified Dec. 31, 2014. http://users.humboldt.edu/ogayle/hist383/Discovery.html. Print – p. 1-2.
11 Ibid. p. 3.
12 Hittell, Theodore Henry (1898). *History of California; Vol. 3, Book X, Chap XII – Treatment of Indians (cont.)* San Francisco, CA: J.N. Stone. Pp. 912-17.

native defiance that would put a "brake" on further Spanish exploration... a certain evidence of substantial native hostility; both during Europeans' first contact and during the American pioneer-renowned westward expansion.

According to Charles A. Murdock, a traveler from Boston, Massachusetts to northern California mentioned in his journal that, "In 1827 a party of adventurers started north from Fort Ross for Oregon, following the coast. One Jedidiah Smith, a trapper, was the leader. It is said that Smith River, near the Oregon line, was named for him. Somewhere on the way all but four were reported killed by the Indians. They are supposed to have been the first white men to enter the Humboldt country."[13] It was the Klamath natives whom would slaughter most of Jedidiah Smith's trapping party that year.

Now, some historians would argue that because there was no "official" established Catholic mission in Northern California, that it did not affect the regional native populations. This is a "half-truth." There were no Catholic missions as you would see in Southern California. Instead, there were ranches. These ranches were used for almost the same purposes – minus the religious doctrine. Instead, there, it would serve more as a native town. Further, Native American tribes were notoriously quick to relay important societal events via intertribal communication; such as word of mouth and messages. Indigenous

---

13 Murdock, Charles A. *A Backward Glance at Eighty, Recollections & Comments,*. San Francisco, California: Paul Elder & Co., 1921. http://www.loc.gov/resource/calbk.137.

tribes had the knowledge of Europeans and – in some level of particularity – indigenous tribal history back east of the Rocky Mountains, as well as more recently from the Spanish of Southern California.

Prior to the discovery of gold dust by James W. Marshall on the 24th of January, 1848, there was very minimum contact by any of the peoples from Anglo-Saxon, Celt, or Caucasian ethnicities.[14] They say first impressions are important, it seems the Spanish Monarchy laid out a poor impression. American settlers pioneering to the West had information on what to prepare for and how to do it – and a lot of them barely had enough money to afford the wagon by itself.

---

14 Sedler, K. Ibid., Ch. 5, Para. 9

NEW AMERICAN SETTLERS

MINER'S CODE OF THE KLAMATH RIVER
- MAY 1852 :

"That in all cases of crime committed by Indians, unless the party should be taken in the act, no revenge should be allowed until an investigation by the neighborhood should take place; that the delivery of the aggressors should be demanded of the nearest ranches, and after a reasonable time given punishment should be inflicted as follows: for murder by the destruction of the ranch to which the criminal belonged and its inhabitants if known.

If not known, by that of those nearest the spot. For theft, by destruction of the ranch or such lighter punishment as should be awarded, but life not to be taken except for stealing horses or in preventing robbery. The punishment of a thief when taken to be in other cases whipping, not to exceed 39 lashes; and cutting the hair.

Offenses of whites against Indians, whether by killing without cause, burning ranches or otherwise, to be punished (at) ....the discretion of a jury, as also the sale of firearms and ammunition to the Indians."[15]

American's like to speculate. They did so very liberally in land property. This circle of speculation and land buying ended in an abrupt stop with the Panic of 1837. An economic depression would follow this event. Americans would end up losing everything they earned and had. Homes and physical property gone. This whole process of financial collapse enabled the desire for new opportunity and adventure. A new climate, environment and life. This is what many people would claim the antidote to their personal and family problems back east

The finding of gold dust particles on January 24th of 1848 in the mountains of the Trinity's caused a famous gold rush. This event changed the native perception of American settlers. Gold miners would end up pouring into the river regions of Northern California. The newcomers to the soon to be new State would end up being told that they were posing a serious problem to the native inhabitants annual ceremonies and rituals, particularly their cultural salmon harvests and acorn gathering parties. The miners who were located in the region were considered more transient and temporary, because of districts set-up to support the small mining communities than anything in regards to regional status.

---

15 Albert Hurtado, *Indian Survival on the California Frontier* (New Haven and London: Yale University Press, 1988) 119-120

Daniel L. Smith

As soon as word hit the rest of the country back East, it started a flood of emigration out West. 1848 and 1849 was good business in Peoria, Illinois for Gregg Carr who stated, "...ironing off California wagons intended to cross the plains the following summer. At that time the whole West was in a blaze. Everybody had the California fever." To understand the pioneers from the 1840's is to understand their upbringings. Those were past times of equal poverty spread regionally across America. Those in the rural regions especially were living in some of the crudest conditions imaginable compared to contemporary living.

Homemade clothes and small wages were a normal part of life. Portions were small, and the hours of obligation and responsibility were incredibly long. The idea of stumbling onto some gold for quick riches was an easy enticement for these settlers. Mining men, loggers, soldiers, laborers, and people fleeing their criminal past; these were the main characters found in these settlements on the newly established Humboldt Bay. Union (Arcata) was the forefront leader of leading mercantile business on Humboldt Bay, making it a well-established original western town

When the American settlers began to establish the timber and fishing industries on the coastal areas of Northern California, they were intent on keeping their settlements separate from the local tribal villages. There was an organic sense to stay separate, given the times past of Native American encounters with American's back east. The history of difficult relations was of course common knowledge within American society at this time. And of course both native and settler wouldn't be so optimistic, or even sure of a different outcome this time around.

Over 250,000 Americans went westward to the gold state between 1841 and 1869. Most people emigrated for other reasons than gold however. Saying goodbye to family and friends is always a hard emotional experience, however, these new emigrants to California would be doing something that has not been done before since the Mayflower. Over 100,000 men were employed as miners, which with high competition for gold would have only turned out to just under $600 per person annually. Interesting note here, that because of local gold inflation – even buying food could become a financial burden.

One miner in the foothills explained, "The price of provisions had become so high that our paltry earnings were not nearly sufficient to pay for the food we required to keep us alive." Another man thought he was doing great if his cost of food dropped to $1.50 a day. During shortages, food prices skyrocketed. Financial burdens on the miners were many, and certainly not many people reaped that gold dream they were aiming for.

These men rarely looked back east after making their journey. It seems that news wouldn't be successful in traveling back east with the harsh realities of gold finding. Historian Oscar Lewis has mentioned that "fewer than one out of twenty California gold seekers returned home richer than when they left. They expressed their frustration in the names of ramshackle mining camps like Poverty Hill, Skunk Gulch, and Hell's Delight."

Americans deciding to take the long road west for a new life would have to figure out how to get there. Overland travel would be the most common way to get to Northern California. This would be done by ways of the Oregon Trail as well as the California Trail. This trek would have taken 90 to 180 days. They encountered 40 miles of dry, dusty and barren desert during the journey and then pushed over the Sierra Nevada mountain range. The terrain and climate were always the issue at the forefront.

During the 3-6 months journey on the California Trail, the wagon was the emigrant's home. Contrary to Hollywood, traveling families would not ride in the wagons because of discomfort. The oxen, horse, and mule pulled wagons did not have suspension to absorb any shock from the rigid terrain. It was very important that the wagon load was as light as possible, so that their train animals did not become overly tired and worn out – which was a problem at times.

The animals that were carried as part of the pack train (beside oxen, mules and horses) were extremely importance to the lives of the settlers too. Without them, they would have died of starvation. Cows, goats, chickens, sheep... they all traveled the trail. Planning for travel would have been the most difficult, as even beyond the trail supplies were very expensive and even unavailable in northern California.

It was the emphasis in keeping a light load that would force settlers to rely heavily on the land and its natural resources along the trail westward. A simple given in life – if you do not eat, you quickly die. This essential survival method of living off the land during travel would end up straining relations with the natives along the path west.

In the time that the California Trail was being used by Americans, the relationship dynamic with the native tribes changed. It was extremely dangerous in the early days of traveling into California. Native Americans were the biggest fear of the entire journey. An unfortunate reality in the truths behind the travel west. In the travels to California, settlers would at times come across peaceful natives who wanted to trade supplies. Metal pots, pans, beads, bullets, and clothing were commonly sought by the local tribes.

Settlers would come to appreciate trading for food, acting as guides, and moccasin shoes. As time went on and people began settling along the path west to California, relations between both parties again, became strained. In the new beginnings of California's discovery, rowdy miners, hell bent on gold and riches were seen as "bent on native destruction" because of indigenous naivety to property claims. In regard to these lawless miners, they were very much only a small minority of the state's population.

California would yield only poverty and disappointment. Alonzo Delano, who traveled far and wide through

Daniel L. Smith

Northern California and its mountainous regions during the gold rush, offered this personal observation:

"Wherever we turned, we met with disappointed and disheartened men, and the trails and mountains were alive with those whose hopes had been blasted, whose fortunes had been wrecked, and who now, with empty pockets and weary limbs, were searching for new diggings, or for employment—hoping to get enough to live on, if nothing more. Some succeeded, but hundreds, after months and years of toil, still found themselves pining for their homes, in misery and want, and with a dimmed eye and broken hopes."[16]

The observations of Mr. Delano ran parallel to that of the disgusted U.S Army officers on California's general personal morals... "utterly arrests the course of civil law."[17] These transient miners of the Klamath and Trinities in search for riches, succumbed to self-centered personal vice, in place of true moral principles. With truth to be told, it truly was the criminal acts of a few (both miners, and native) that exacerbated a regional conflict.

.The people who actually made it out to Northern California, were ones who were well informed of the

---

16 Delano, A. 1854. Life on the Plains and among the Diggings. Auburn, NY: Miller, Orton & Mulligan. Reprint, Alexandria, VA: Time-Life Books, 1981.
17 Ltrs., Pacific Division, Record Group 393, National Archives Building. National Archives Microcopy. Wool to Thomas, Aug. 14, 1855; Townsend to Judah, Aug 30, 1855.; Jones to Buchanan, Oct. 18, 1855, RG393, NA.

"Indian" troubles they were probably going to encounter. Communication in getting out West to Northern California was prudent. Without solid communication would mean certain failure for means of survival. It was solid documentation on the travels that kept the settlers well informed for that era.

Alonzo Delano would further write in 1849:

"For Intelligence, they are far behind the Indians east of the Rocky Mountains, but although they are affectionate and kind to each other, as is the custom among all civilized tribes, their women are held to be inferior to males, and are reduced to unmitigated slavery. The men are idle vagabonds, and spend most of their time lounging, occasionally shooting birds and small game, or spearing fish, and, as it seemed to me, more for amusement than from any desire to be useful to their families....

"The Indians of California are more swarthy in complexion and of smaller stature than those east of the Rocky Mountains; and although they may be placed in situations where they will fight bravely, they are less bold, and more cowardly in the main, than those on the Great Plains west of the Missouri; while they are more gentile in their natures, and become willing slaves to those who will feed and clothe them, if they are not overworked. They have more of the Asiatic cast of countenances than the eastern tribes, and are easily controlled if properly managed. Strict justice, and a uniform but firm and gentle behavior, will conciliate them, and gain their goodwill and respect."[18]

Thomas Woodward, an American settler, wrote in his personal diary of his travels of his native dilemmas in 1850, and while crossing the mountainous trails of Northern California country he wrote:

"These Mountains is infested By Savages of The most cruel and Theifish Propensities which Require The Most vigalent attention To keep Them from stealing your stock where They cannot do This..."

Mr. Woodward was explaining how the natives had a propensity for malicious and harassing behavior, in this case the property theft. He continues...

"...They will crawl among The Sage and wound your horses and mules with Their arrows so That you may be compeled To leave Them That they may get Their flesh To eat..."

The natives were skilled at stealth when stalking and harassing the settlers moving West. They would take aim for the wagon horses and mules, knowing the logistical importance, as a distraction method for meeting the ends of stealing cattle for their meat (interesting to note that cattle was not native to the Northern California region). Woodward carries on in his diary...

"...some horses was stole last night from a camp a little above us and we had not Traveled over a mile when

---

18 Robt. F. Heizer, Alan J. Almquist, *The Other Californians, Prejudice and Discrimination under Spain, Mexico, and the U.S. to 1920*(Berkeley: University of California Press), 23.

we came To a camp where There was a sight That was sufficient To make any man if feeling sweare eternal vengeance against every Red Skin in The country..."

Mr. Woodward and his party made camp, and they awoke to some horses stolen from the pack. His party geared up for travel (minus the handful of horses), and one-mile in, came across a camp. A fellow settler from a preceding party lie dying in agony with an arrow through his lower heart. Woodward goes on...

"...a Poor fellow by The name of Samuel Oliver from near Milwaukee Wisconsin had been on guard – They shot an arrow Trough The lower Part of the mans heart with That force That The head of The arrow still Remained in him – he was Dying and his comrades was swearing vengeance – They Brought him Down To River to Bury – we incamped for The night after Traveling a few Miles Down the Bottom having made about 20 Miles Today."

Samuel Oliver was a pioneer from Milwaukee, Wisconsin. He was standing lone guard overnight for his wagon party. He was surprise attacked and killed by an arrow through the heart in the early morning hours by an unknown native band. His party mourned with vengeance. The comradery of the settling American family and neighbors, through the bitingly harsh travel to Northern California, especially during the days of the infamous Gold Rush was certainly a bonding experience.

BAD APPLES

There seems to have been a cultural predisposition to war and its direct connection within California's indigenous tribal population with the Spanish Europeans settling into California. Spanish territorial California was oppressive and pressed upon the natives; as established above. The other connection to this hostile approach towards California settlers from the East, is the systematic targeting of settlers (civilians), which often followed more conventional assaults. There is enough evidence established that California's Northern tribes were justified in their uncomfortable and not so hospitable feelings towards any new settlers and settlement. Consider Spanish empiricism, as well as American settlement back East.

We face two solid facts. First, the humble truth is Native Americans did target civilians for murder; and secondly, there was absolutely no pre-existent consensus among whites that all Native Americans deserved such treatment or ill-conduct. Such an example speaks from an article from the Sacramento Union, written to the editor by early California settlers. They mentioned their feelings given due to native displacement by settlers.

They saw it truly as the responsibility of the U.S. government to assist in a completely peaceful transition for the indigenous.[19] So as such, the ideals of those who have perverted the truths of humane and moral treatment towards others, are also the ones who ended up the societal outcasts themselves back on the eastern side of the Mississippi.

As far as the natives of the 18th and 19th century were concerned, doing wrong was generally seen as being harmful to the tribe as a group rather than the individual person. This could be against another person, or group, regardless of culture. It would not be unreasonable to assume that if a tribe has a more war-like custom and demeanor attached to its particular society, that its groups of families which keep the native societies customs would have essentially took away some form of personal accountability. This eliminates a certain moral responsibility to self, enabling opportunity for vices; further dissolving personal self-control not to commit depredations against others.

This author would like to make it absolutely clear that not all native tribes were "war-like" in this manner, however, all native tribes did practice cultural customs completely opposite to traditional American society. Those American societal traditions are based upon Judeo-Christian beliefs and English-styled common laws in

---

19 *The Beacon*. "The Digger Indian Reservations, and C." December 15, 1858, pp. 1, col 6., article 1., vol. 2, no. 39.

government. Regardless of how deep the cultural analysis of both the natives and settlers – each side had "bad apples" that were already blind to all form of cultural or religious moral and human decency. This claim is evident through documented weak personal choices, lack of apparent self-control, and a clearly displayed opportunistic show of criminal behavior for personal gain.[20]

Many of the "bad apples" of the settling bunch came from the criminal elements of American society as mentioned before. A lot of these men were old experienced and weathered men. These men unfortunately had no problems treating the natives like stray dogs. They typically held a wicked disposition towards the natives of the county. It is a negative aspect of any society, to have such an evil, such as a group of individuals set out to exploit the majority of society attempting to live by the rules.

Some of these individual criminal elements would end up turning into roving bands of "unprincipled whites,"[21] hellbent of exploiting both natives and settlers. Done by false rumors, unfair trade, false agreements, robbery, violence, and the list could continue. This in turn creates an endless social cycle of retaliatory outbreaks. Clearly this adds an element of insecurity and chaos to the lives of those choosing to live fair minded. An eye-for-an eye

---

20 Carp, Robert A., and Ronald Stidham. *Judicial Process in America*, 9th ed. Washington, DC: SAGE, 2001.
21 "The Honey Lake Troubles – Another U.S. Fort Wanted." *San Francisco Bulletin*, 28 October 1857

and a tooth-for-a-tooth found serious emphasis among the natives of northern California.[22]

The natives were suspicious and watchful, they seemed to magnify all little trespasses into much larger complaints to the settlers. One of the characteristics of the communal-style of culture that Native Americans exhibit, is that they cannot distinguish and particularize between individuals. The result of this cultural communal process: if a settler killed a native tribesman, the native would retaliate and kill the first settler he caught – regardless of any fact the true perpetrator to the murder got caught or not.

It was this reality that cultural tradition that would cause a number of somber difficulties and conflicts encountered by the early incoming settlers of Humboldt County. A newspaper from Portland, Maine even stated that the natives were "very bad" at Thunderboldt (Humboldt) Bay in California.[23] Several white men had been murdered by natives between Humboldt and Yreka, just under two months prior to that press release.[24]

Moral boundaries could be an argument on its own. For the sake of this literature, I will aim to look at the cultural norms and "not-so-norms" through the lens of the American settler in Humboldt County in the mid-1800s.

---

22 Sedler, K. Ibid., Ch. 8, Para. 2
23 *Daily National Democrat*. "Portland Maine Transcript." October 26, 1858, pp. 2, col 1. Vol. 1, no. 63.
24 *Daily National Democrat*. "Untitled." August 19, 1858, pp. 2, col 3., vol. 1, no. 7.

It would seem native social differences were presenting themselves at every corner. Around the 10th of January, 1860, Mrs. R. F. Herrick, a resident of Union (Arcata) recalled an incident where a local native by the name of "Sore Eyed Tom", a large man by stature, coincidently snuck into her house in broad daylight while her husband was away on local business.

The native man, completely naked aside from his 2-foot knife hanging from the leather strap around his neck, asked for "whago (white) bread." She responded that she "did not have any bread ready." Sore Eyed Tom replied, "Too much lie." At that point while in the middle of slicing potatoes she thought his presence, while being briefly patient – unbearable, and chased him off with her knife.[25] I have gone a bit ahead here to give the reader a little insight on the conditions in Union as first-hand testimony given by Mrs. Herrick herself.

The conditions in Union were typical of any other town on Humboldt Bay. From 1851 to 1854, societal changes were slowly taking place in the region and economically building up a major trading port for the mid-19th century California. It was above the bay area, in the mountains that mining activities spurred economic activity in the area. It was a long transition from mining operations, to farming and timber, that Humboldt would slowly shift into formal American society.

---

25 Sedler, K. "History of Humboldt County, California" Ch. 8, Para. 9-10

1845-1870 An Untold Story of Northern California

As the county of Humboldt would finally organize in 1853, and by 1854 Union would have fourteen different stores and businesses. Grocery; wholesale and retail; hotels; drug stores; churches; saddle and harness makers; gunsmiths; jewelers... among the handful to name. It was a boomtown at that time to say the least. It was only in the earlier simple mining communities above Humboldt, that there was a population large enough to sufficiently defend against the depredations of local natives. They were "quite savage." The mining populations numbers kept their assets secured through the harshness of winters as well.

Agricultural communities began to grow, although they started out very small. Roads started as trails. The Redwood forests thick and sometimes impassable. Rivers treacherous. Soon the lumber, farming, and fishing industries began to develop. Eventually, these industries would serve to clear the land for more permanent housing, farming, fishing, and typical business. With all population growth comes it's lesser elements.

Crime is bound to happen in such an unforgiving and seemingly lawless place so far West. Opportunity was abound for the lawless individual in rugged Northern California. For the bad apples coming from back east, they were experiencing severe economic and social hardships. The economy was fractured between 1845 and throughout the Civil War. Politics were shattered. As was the infrastructure. As was the nation.

UNSTABLE CALIFORNIA

The original pioneers of Northern California were content with the difficulties presented to them, as danger lurked around every single moment. A real life "choose-your-own-adventure" if you will. In regards to the American pioneer, every obstruction presented to them provided by the great wilds of nature were consistently overcame through perseverance. Every danger present within the depredations between the natives of Northern California and the American settlers; are evidenced in texts as a form of deterrence and discouragement.

However like all societies around the world and throughout all of time, both the natives and settlers had a handful of "bad apples," or, "lost souls." And regardless of opinion, these people were blind to every form of cultural moral and human civility in their personal capacity. It truly was in these times, the native population of Northern California was the majority to that of the settlers from the American east. It is absolutely impossible to know the true numbers of the Americans settling the Humboldt region due to the population instability.

1845-1870 An Untold Story of Northern California

The Native American population during these early years presented, had not yet received any communication from the U.S. Government to shift to reservations. Their native ranches were a more permanent foundation for them. Almost serving as a native town of sorts. Their numbers had not been reduced by death, or disease, and there was absolutely zero restrictions on their human liberties, as well as their methods of living.[26] At this point, the U.S. Government itself never even came close to targeting the native population for extermination.[27] It was here that purely culture and humanity would be used to navigate the often surprising encounters between native tribes and settlers.

At the 1st California State Constitutional Convention, those assembled voted to eliminate the Indians' right to vote because they were not U.S. Constitutionally protected persons. Further, they lacked permanent citizenship rights as non-citizens. In 1850, the "Act for the Government and Protection of Indians" was enacted by the first session of the State Legislature. This act of legislation would of course set the tone for further strained Native-Settler relations.

The new policy provided for the following:
1. The Justice of the Peace would have jurisdiction over all complaints between Indians and Whites;

---

26 Ellison, W. H. (1922). The Federal Indian Policy in California, 1846-1860. *The Mississippi Valley Historical Review*, 9(1), 37. doi:10.2307/1886099
27 Fletcher, Matthew L.M., *American Indian Tribal Law*. N.p.: Aspen Publishing, 2011.

"but in no case shall a white man be convicted of any offense upon the testimony of an Indian or Indians."
2. Landowners would permit Indians who were peaceably residing on their land to continue to do so.
3. Whites would be able to obtain control of Indian children
4. If any Indian was convicted of a crime, any White person could come before the court and contract for the Indian's services, and in return, would pay the Indian's fine.
5. It would be illegal to sell or administer alcohol to Indians.
6. Indians convicted of stealing a horse, mule, cow, or any other valuable could receive any number of lashes not to exceed 25, and fines not to exceed $200. (It should be noted that the law provided that abusing an Indian child by Whites was to be punished by no more than a $10 fine. It is hard to compare the penalty with the crime.)
7. Any Indian found strolling, loitering where alcohol was sold, begging, or leading a profligate course of life would be liable for arrest. The justice, mayor, or recorder would make out a warrant. Within 24 hours, the services of the Indian in question could be sold to the highest bidder. The term of service would not exceed four months.[28]

---

28 *Ibid.*

This state law of California was abused by some entrepreneurial landholders in regards to the use of native laborers. One exception to note: the law did allow natives to live on privately owned land. This practice of indentured servitude in California made it a legality for these natives to be "locked down" for longer periods of time. The law also allowed for this practice to be initiated at a younger age. Ten years after the law of 1850 was exacted, it was amended. It stated that, "Indian children and any vagrant Indian could be put under the custody of Whites for the purpose of employment and training. Under the law, it was possible to retain the service of Indians until 40 years of age for men and 35 years of age for women."[29]

It would be of the utmost fairness to state that; not in the defense of, or to find an excuse for, the application of oppressive laws pressed upon the native peoples of Northern California. The point of view of whom actually utilized the piece of legislation authorizing indentured servitude in payment for perceived crimes against the settling populace of the region would be found in two categories: One, slave owning southerners who's lively hoods and business made their slave culture in California relevant. Two, criminal elements within the settling society (there were a lot!) who would have found the lack of heart for another human being to make dirty ends meet.

It's important to note too that political boundaries in the state were both equally divided Union and

---

29 *Ibid.*

Confederate in ideologies. Regardless of an individual's personal viewpoint, the fact of the matter states that the United States of America was in a Civil War. Slavery was still relevant, as well as a war that men were dying over to abolish. It would be extremely unreasonable to isolate California as it's "own brand" of society, with its "own problems," when national issues such as racial slavery was still a serious issue.[30] The United States of America was knee deep in its own societal problems, and the settlers would learn quickly that social and legal cultural issues will follow them, wherever they emigrate too.

Newspaper "Alta California," would report in 1862: "Little more than a hundred miles from San Francisco, in Mendocino County, the practice of Indian stealing is still extensively carried out. Only recently, George H. Woodman was caught near Ukiah with sixteen Indian children, as he was about to take them out of the county for sale. It is well known that a number of men in that region had for years made it their profession to capture and sell unfortunate juveniles, the price ranging from $30 to $150 depending on their quality."[31]

It was in the 1860's, that the U.S. Government would initiate the "Peace Policy" as its first emphasized focus on acculturation – or simply absorbing the culture as a form of tolerance. This mission would be accomplished mainly

---

30 Walters, Ronald. *American Reformers, 1815-1860*. (Hill and Wayne, NY. Revised Edition) p. 7.
31 Harrison, Michael. "Indian Problem Today." Paper, Sonoma State College. 1966.

1845-1870 An Untold Story of Northern California

by focused "cultural exchange."[32] In doing so, it would introduce tribal culture to American culture, and vis versa. This would further open up native understanding to American familiarity and the moral parameters of living. This policy would also prove the Christian ethic in American culture (which is what American culture is legally based upon[33]); where cultural absorption and tolerance precedes ethnic extermination by any and all means.[34]

President Fillmore would send eighteen treaties to be ratified by the U.S. Senate in February of 1852. The California state senators were recognized in their legislation, and the whole U.S. Senate would go into closed-door meetings for further examination of the treaties involved with the local natives. The treaties would not be passed by Congress on the senate floor and the files were placed on the side. They would sit out of view until 53 years later, when in 1871 Congress would state that the government would no longer deal or negotiate treaties with Native Americans. The U.S. Government failed to ratify the treaties, however; it did continue the policy of setting up reservations and moving the local native

---

32 Guéno, M. P. (2017). Native Americans, Law, and Religion in America. *Oxford Research Encyclopedia of Religion*, pp. 7-8. doi:10.1093/acrefore/9780199340378.013.140

33 Lutz, Donald, "The Relative Influence of European Writers on Late 18th Century American Political Thought," *American Political Science Review*, LXXXVIII (1984) p. 189-197.

34 Beliles, M. A., & McDowell, S. K. (2010). The Christian Form of Our Government. In *America's Providential History* (3rd ed., p. 186). The Providence Foundation.

tribes to them in defense of American interests of life and property.

To understand the pioneer of the American West, you must understand where their mindset is directed. We do this by looking at three different aspects of the pioneer culture of the mid-1800's. To get to this point, we must back up a bit in time to when the United States of America broke from England as a colony. These Americans had little empirical evidence and no scientific evidence to support their beliefs, nothing in fact but faith. One shouldn't be mind-blown to think that over 150 years ago, Christian tradition was commonplace.

These types of activities occurred until 1866, when, to comply with the 14th Amendment of the United States Constitution, the State Legislature repealed the law. The 14th Amendment provides that no state should infringe on any citizen's "privileges or immunities" nor "deprive any person of life, liberty, or property without due process of law," nor deny to any person "the equal protection of the law."

Pioneer George Bonniwell, made a journal entry proving his personal faith:

"We have nothing for breakfast but a little tea. Hard times. We was on our march a little after sunrise. Went along the foot of the mountain and now our poor horses, while I write this, is struggling up a steep mountain. They are almost up. God help and supply our wants. These words strengthen me this morning. Put thy trust in the Lord and he will strengthen thine heart. Yes, Lord, I will though thou shows me. Blessed be God, my soul is happy. My lord, pour thy spirit upon me and let they grace sustain me. We descended the mountain and had a beautiful prospect of the surrounding mountains."[35]

It is in the late 18th century that America was founded as a Christian nation and would begin to see an emergence of a people who would leave the churches. This would also cause a societal 'bend' in moral and ethical teachings and move forward in time with a "go with the flow" attitude of society; namely one like "being your own man" and "making your own way." However this thought process would end up being a fallacy, and also the start to moral and ethical decline in American society. Unbelief to Divine accountability, corruption of doctrine, and neglect of its institutions; all necessary for the genuine prosperity America has come to know.

In knowing that the colonial United States was a Christian nation both legally and in character, later into the 1800's a competing ideology emerged in American society called socialism. A philosophy which has been tactically successful. In the late 1800's, Christian ideology began to be neglected in the public school system as well. Science was no longer being taught in a reasonable way; and Christianity then became some irrelevant religious dogma, taught in the schools to poverty level and middle-class children.

---

35 "The Gold Rush Diary of George Bonniwell - August/September, 1850." Emigrant Road - Friday Aug 9 and 120 days out. Accessed April 20, 2019. https://www.emigrantroad.com/gold05.html.

This neglect opened a space to be eventually filled by a competing ideology – Darwin and his theory of evolution. Karl Marx wrote his alternative theory book in 1844. Marx's book actually never had much influence on American society as a whole until the nation took a backslide from ethical economics and turned to materialism and greed. This materialist concept continued to grow throughout America ever since. It was the cultural ideological shift in mid-19th century America, that set the tone for morality and ethics preceding the settling of Northern California.

For the Americans of the 19th century back east, the division and removal of traditional Christian ethic, led to an increase in immoral and unethical activity within society. Americans have typically been less restricted to traditions, because the American sense of heritage includes revolution and republicanism. It was really this world-view that gave the pioneers of the mid-1800's a real unique feeling of being a new and unique people.

TRIBAL CUSTOMS & RELIGION

Native Americans of Northern California are spiritual in their beliefs, which are also known as Animist. These native cultures live their lives governed by the thought that doing, or not doing something, and that these behaviors could affect your future as a living and breathing person. Inevitably with this belief you would develop a constant sense of fear that you would bring harm or misfortune upon yourself, as well as your family.

This is what it is like to live among Animists. Natives believe that spirit beings are directly responsible for everything that happens, good and bad. The only reasonable approach to this perceived reality is to do everything you can to keep those spirit beings happy. Most of them hold to a belief in one supreme deity who is the creator of all that is. Differing varieties of myths regarding creation and how man came to be are regional. All tribes however believe in one all mighty creator. The native creator could be described as deistic.

Then there are Demi-gods (good spirits/angels), lesser gods (bad spirits), nature spirits (typically neutral), ancestral spirits (generally good, but can be bad), humans, pre-human (un-reincarnated spirits).³⁶ This is the Animist cosmology of hierarchy. As you can see, there is a god-like similarity in native belief to the One Creator, which almost parallels the belief of the Christian God of most American society pre-20th century.

In regard to moral sin (or doing wrongs, committing crimes), Animists generally dwell in corporate or tribal social surroundings; that is to say that they are more concerned with the group than the individual. Concepts of evil are actually based upon what is toxic to the tribe as a whole element. David Weber explained, that "... Indians only cooperated when they believed that they had something to gain from the new religion and the material benefits that accompanied it, or too much to lose from resisting."³⁷ Animists have no guilt because they have transgressed against the Creator, however will sense shame if their actions are seen harmful or negative to the tribe.

Exhibiting certain social behaviors that bring the fury of the spirits – such as breaking with customs, or failing proper rituals – is considered evil.³⁸ It is because of this that the tribe may act to punish an offender. Further, shame and fear are constantly employed to motivate

---

36 Hodge, Bodie, and Roger Patterson. "Animism (Spiritism)." In *World Religions & Cults Volume 2: Moralistic, Mythical and Mysticism Religions*, pp. 230. Green Forest : New Leaf Publishing Group, 2016.
37 David J. Weber, *The Spanish Frontier in North America* (New Haven: Yale University Press, 1992), p. 115.
38 Ibid. p. 232

individuals to comply with social expectations. For the Animist, iniquity is not a violation against the Creator, but one's social group. Right and wrong are not issues of personal morality, but of their practical effect on the tribe as a whole element.

There is no central founder of animism. There are no universal writings or sacred manuscripts that are common to animist peoples, and if there is any literature, it is locally written. In fact, because animism is associated with tribal peoples and no written language, their myths and traditions are passed down orally, or word-of-mouth.[39] This tradition is typical of world tribal cultures located well outside of civilized societies.

The religious specialists of animist societies included at least one, if not all of the following: Priest, Medicine Man, Shaman, Witch, Sorcerer, Medium. Of those listed, we will focus on the Medicine Man; whose name is given to some in animist societies whose job is to attempt to use magic and spirit manipulation to bring healing and other beneficial properties to those in spiritual need, and in sickness. The following is an expert from a cultural event that had occurred between the settlers and local native tribe to Northern California on Wednesday the 13th, August 1858:

"A very delicate crisis in the matrimonial history of an Indian Chiefs wife, ("hips tyee Klootchman) whose

---

39 Philip M. Steyne, *Gods of Power: A Study in the Beliefs and Practices of Animists* (Columbia, SC: Impact International Foundation, 2011), pp. 72.

residence adjoins our office, occurred on Wednesday evening, between the hours of nine and eleven o'clock...

...An infernal howling, beating of tin pans, grunting and " ooh-oohing," induced us, in question the mood, to repair to the scene, to inquire the cause, and if possible bring it to an abrupt termination. A curious multitude, thronging around the shanty, enabled us with difficulty to get a peep at the mysterious proceedings going on within...

... we arrived at the door of the lodge, in the center of which we discovered the "medicine man," or accoucheur, dipping his hands into a basin of water : rubbing them together, a la Lady Macbeth ; thrusting his arms out stiffly before him ; gnashing his teeth ; contorting his features; bending his forehead down to the earth ; wriggling his body, and agonizing generally in so violent and strange a manner, as to start great drops of sweat on his brow...

... In front of him a bright tire was burning, into which he had thrust several bones, howling a sort of tune or incantation in the meantime, to which a chorus was made by some half dozen other Indians, lying or sitting on the ground, heating a kind of drum, and the ground, and several tin vessels with sticks, producing a noise similar to what might be imagined appropriate to pandemonium...

... At intervals the doctor uttered an "ooh-ooh!" when the howling instantly censed. He would look gravely into the fire for a moment, fill his mouth with water from the basin in front of him, and drawing this drapery aside from the body of the submissive patient, (stretched out on a mat by his side,) spurt it upon her naked bosom. Then would recommence the clatter which was prolonged as above stated, when they suddenly ceased...

... Next morning, on looking into the shanty we did no discover, that there was any addition to the number of occupants. On the contrary, doctor, patient and chorus, had disappeared ; and our fervent hope is, that they may never return again; at least to this neighborhood."
— Whatcom Northern Light, Aug 14.

"Dr. Jack," was a native medicine man whom his tribe believed to hold supernatural abilities. Dr. Jack was also killed by his tribe because of these "powers," which is common among differing native tribes.[40] As part of many native American cultures, the ritualistic killing of their own medicine men is part of their own cultural laws.[41]

This press release originated as a first-hand experience from the settlers viewpoint during a tribal ritual; with the emphasis of healing. Nobody that is animist by practice can give a concrete account on the Creation of Man. The following was an account orally narrated by a tribe located near the Lassen region of Northern California, "A mountain lion and wild cat were brothers living together. They became estranged, each had been dependent upon the other. A beautiful ball was found in the

---

40 "A Judicial Farce." *Lassen Advocate*, 12 August 1897, page 2, col. 1. (vol. 31, no. 47)

41 "Indians as Healers." *Oroville Register,* 21 July 1887, col. 1, col. 2 & 3.(vol. 10, no. 44) "Indian Medicinal Ideas" &"The Indian Medicine Man" [Globe Democrat]

river by two girls and the next morning... it was man."⁴² Nothing can be said about the true origins of this myth, as tribal cultures story of human existence varies from tribe to tribe.

In context, it would not be unusual of a typical mid-19th century American to have felt awkward, uneasy, untrusting, or hostile towards these tribal spiritual beliefs and customs. Religion is always tied into the legal doctrine of the relevant nation. Every single nation on earth has a national government based upon regional religious principles, and cultural laws. Father Paul le Jeune, a former professor of rhetoric at the universities of Nevers and Caen, had stated of his personal experiences and the transliteration of their native languages in 1634:

"...all words which refer to the regulation and government of a city, Province, or Empire; all that concerns justice, reward and punishment ... all these things are never found either in the thoughts or upon the lips of the Savages."⁴³

It seems fairly doubtful if native people could even comprehend the meaning of "private property", "buying and selling", or "theft" in the context of personal relations within their community – tribe, band, clan, or family.

---

42 "The Indians' Account of the Creation of Man." *Lassen Advocate*, 6 April 1872, col. 4 col. 2. (vol. 7, no. 39)
43 JR, vol. 6, p. 101; vol. 7, p. 21; Leon Pouliot, "Paul le Jeune:, *DCB*, Lucien Campeau, "Pierre Biard", *Dictonary of Canadian Biography* (hereafter *DCB)* Toronto: University of Toronto Press, 1966-1994), vol. 1, pp. 453-458.

Even earlier French observers stationed in the United States didn't think indigenous peoples could clearly recognize private property rights either.[44] Evidence is further established by a letter to the British Consulate by a Spanish Provincial Governor of California via Santa Barbara. In this letter, the Spanish Governor was worried about provincial protection and foreign aid from Britain. This would be because they were afraid of the hostility and economic damage from the local natives and the established Bear Flag Movement.[45]

Sonoma historian Peter Meyerhof said, "There were rumors of the Native Americans being stirred up by the (Mexican) Californios to burn the crops of the settlers."[46] These unsettling rumors of hostile intentions are evidence that would further push the American settlers to the defense of their homesteads at whatever the cost. The fact of the matter is, the indigenous natives were responsible for burning American settlers crops and homesteads. However, just how involved the Mexican Californios were in rabble rousing the indigenous natives

---

44 Ibid. *JR*, vol. 3, p. 195)
45 Wainwright, Mary-Jo. 1996. "Milestones in California History: The 1846 Bear Flag Revolt: Early Cultural Conflict in California." *California History* 75 (2): 25177573-25177573. Accessed 5 8, 2019. http://ch.ucpress.edu/content/75/2/25177573.
46 Posner, Russel M. "A British Consular Agent in California: The Reports of James A. Forbes. 1843-1846." *Southern California Quarterly*, Vol. 53, No. 2 (UCP: JUNE 1971), p. 110. Accessed March 29th 2019. https://www.jstor.org/stable/41170342

would remain just rumors, as no evidence has surfaced proving otherwise.

According to Pamela Preston, "Native American, Alaskan Indian, and Native Hawaiian societies have traditionally used intoxicating substances in religious rituals, the introduction of alcoholic beverages by European explorers and settlers in the New World can be considered the beginning of substance abuse by the Indigenous people of the United States."[47] On the contrary though. The truth is that before the year 1492 Native Americans actually brewed different kinds of alcoholic drinks. Alcohol has been made since the dawn of creation. In the Cradle of Civilization (or the Middle East), archeologists have found physical proof that "brewing of beer was an important aspect of feasting and society in the Late Epipaleolithic era" (12,000-9,500 BC).[48] As the early peoples only possessed stone tools and basic technology, clearly it doesn't take much to make a simple alcoholic drink.[49]

This was certainly the case in North America. Before the first contacts with European colonists, alcohol was

---

47 Preston, Pamela. "Native Americans and Substance Abuse." In *Encyclopedia of Race and Crime*, edited by Helen T. Greene and Shaun L. Gabbidon, 590-592. Thousand Oaks, CA: SAGE Publications, Inc., 2009. doi: 10.4135/9781412971928.n237
48 How Beer Gave Us Civilization." The New York Times. Last modified October 19, 2018. http://www.nytimes.com/2013/03/17/opinion/sunday/how-beer-gave-us-civilization.html?_r=0.
49 "'World's oldest brewery' found in cave in Israel, say researchers". *BBC*. Last modified September 15, 2018. https://www.bbc.com/news/world-middle-east-45534133.

made and used mostly in the southwestern United States. This would differ by tribe, as some would brew weak beers, wine and other fermented drinks. Some of these drinks would be made stronger (8-14% ABV) but were typically only used for ceremonial and spiritual purposes. How the indigenous Americans prepared and distilled these more potent drinks are still unknown today. The distillation technique required to make stronger, potent forms of alcohol were unknown. However, it is well documented that Mexican Native Americans made well over forty different types alcoholic drinks from many different types of plant substances: honey, palm sap, wild plum, and pineapple.[50]

In the Southwest United States...

The Papago, Piman, Apache and Maricopa all used the saguaro cactus to produce a wine, sometimes called haren a pitahaya. The Coahuiltecan in Texas combined mountain laurel with the Agave plant to create an alcoholic drink, and the Pueblos and Zunis were believed to have made fermented beverages from aloe, maguey, corn, prickly pear, pitahaya and even grapes. Similarly, the Apache fermented corn to make tiswin (also called tulpi and tulapai) and the yucca plant to make a different alcoholic beverage.

On the East Coast of the United States...

---

[50] "Native Americans Were Not Introduced to Alcohol by Europeans." *Today I Found* Out. Last modified November 17, 2013. http://www.todayifoundout.com/index.php/2013/11/native-americans-introduced-alcohol-europeans/.

The Creek Nation of Georgia and Cherokee Nation of the Carolinas used local fruits to make alcohol, and in the Northeast, "there is some evidence that the Huron made a mild beer made from corn. In addition, "despite the fact that they had little to no agriculture, both the Aleuts and Yuit of Alaska were believed to have made alcoholic drinks from fermented berries." Further it is noted that, "Native Americans used a corn precursor to make a brewed drink; they note: "the ancestral grass of modern maize, teosinte, was well suited for making beer – but was much less so for making corn flour."[51]

It should be noted, however, that most of these beverages were relatively weak, presumably no stronger than wine. Whiskey, on the other hand, is usually 60% ABV, and grain alcohol (e.g., moonshine) is often 95% ABV. As a result, when Europeans introduced these stronger drinks, Native Americans were in for a shock. Various Indian culture brewed different drinks according to what was available in the local areas. The Klamath natives fermented alcoholic drinks out of manzanita berries – very tart and acidic. Pamela Preston further goes on to say, "Among some Native American groups, mind-altering substances have spiritual value through the creation of altered states of consciousness."[52], Charles L. Camp, and George C. Yount – both pioneers –emigrated from the east coast of the United States. They wrote a personal

---
51 Ibid., *Today I Found Out*. (Paragraphs 2 – 5.)
52 Ibid., Preston, Pamela. "Native Americans and Substance Abuse."

account regarding the customs of the locals natives of Northern California in 1826:

"The religious customs of all the Tribes on the coast of the Pacific are similar - Their Religion consists chiefly in dancing, strange con torsions of the body & imagined familiarity with good & bad spirits, & the Ghosts of departed friends - All the tribes have their Sweat houses, or Temples to which they resort for all religious rites & ceremonies - These buildings are so constructed that they are capable of being heated like an oven - They creep into these heated houses, & lie around the fire for the healing of all maladies - Many of their cures are effected by dancing around the fire in these houses - Often they dance till they fall senseless –

"Always, in their religious dances, some individuals are appointed to sit & watch those dancing, lest they should fall into the fire & be burned - They will lie till the sweat stands in pools upon the ground - They believe in witchcraft, & that by a certain process of sweating they can bewitch their enemies - When in their religious dances, they become stupefied & fall, they often lie an hour or more, with no other indication of life than the mere beating of the pulse - No one is allowed to molest them then, & when they rise they generally have oracular or preternatural communications to make; to which all listen as they would to communications from heaven –

"They are represented & believed to be communications from supernatural beings, or from the ghosts of departed friends - After thus holding converse with the dead, or with celestial spirits they are very eloquent & tell many strange & wonderful things - If the spirits tell them that they are about to die, they will publish the communication & then invariably lie down in death - If one receive a revelation that one of his kindred, or a neighbor is to die, immediately he will lie down, and expire without a groan or murmur - In their falling at meetings for religious worship, the phenomena of falling resemble those of the Methodists & some other Denominations, in the days of Whitfield, & in subsequent periods in the United States - There is this difference only - The Indians carry the custom farther, & are more extravagant."[53]

---

[53] Camp, Charles L., and George C. Yount. "The Chronicles of George C. Yount: California Pioneer of 1826." *California Historical Society Quarterly* 2, no. 1 (1923): 3-66. http://www.jstor.org.ezproxy.snhu.edu/stable/25177691

NATIVE JUSTICE

Some tribes were known to divvy out communal punishment as a consequence to law breakers. So how did this work? Parents and grandparents of certain tribes did not like to physically discipline their children. Instead, the child or teenager who committed the crime, would be sent to a communal location. Punishment was then dealt out by an elected community representative.[54] In a true psychological sense, this discredits the parents and grandparents and could cause problems within the family when trying to assert parental authority over their young. It is critical to point out that, "Native Americans demographically have a greater proportion of crime-prone individuals, such as young males."[55]

A man had been outside on his homestead when he observed a squaw near his property harvesting strawberry's in a strange position and posture. This man, quietly kept an eye from a distance when he later noticed a male

---

54 Ackerman, L.A. Family instability and juvenile delinquency among Nez Perce's. *American Anthropologist*, 1971, *73*, 595-603.
55 Lester, David., *Crime and the Native American.* eBook Collection (EBSCOhost) Printed: 2/25/2019

native carrying her around on his back. The reason for this; the male native had come home drunk after some time out, and burned his wife's feet. As a punishment for this unfortunate event was carrying her around on his back for the rest of her life. At the end of her life, he would then be put to death by his tribe.[56] It is apparent for the natives of Northern California, there were tribal laws that are to be abided by.

There is a theory that it was the Europeans who faulted Native Americans to endure generations of alcoholism and alcohol abuse. This belief would be a fallacy; as alcohol has been found methodically not playing a major factor in enabling native murder.[57] With this being stated, I also must make note that some indigenous regions have especially high murder rates, and further, there has always been a traditionally high murder rate both before and after reservations were even established.[58] For some tribes according to Professor Goodwin at the University of Chicago, "many of the murders committed by natives were seen as justified; with this also representing retaliation and feud killings."[59]

---

56 "Indian Justice." *Quincy Union*, 31 December 1804, col. 1 col 3. (vol. 3 no. 10)
57 Levy, J. E., & Kunitz, S. J. *Indian Drinking*. New York: Wiley, 1974.
58 Levy, J. E., & Kunitz, S. J. "Indian Reservations, anomie, and social pathologies. *Southwestern Journal of Anthropology,* 1971, 27, 97-128 –
Note: These statements are made on account of lack of empirical evidence pre-Reservation Era for reliable estimates.
59 Goodwin, C., *The Social Organization of the Western Apache*. Chicago: University of Chicago, 1942.

1845-1870 An Untold Story of Northern California

It is important to understand that not all tribes had violent tendencies. Some tribes disapproved of violence and avoided situations that might provoke violence, however, the others would place a high value on their courage, and ferocity. This would be demonstrated through fighting and war if necessary. In the course of Northern California history, it is apparent that half of the tribes were peaceful, while the other half was hostile. The Wintoon (or Redwood Indians), Klamath, Hupa, Yuki, Mad River, Little River and Trinidad (Yurok) natives were all deemed maliciously hostile at some point towards the recently implanted Anglo-American settlers.

The Yuki tribe for example; enjoyed a rich annual round of religious celebrations, social dances, trade expeditions and – war raids. Their reputation was fierce and warlike by their neighboring tribes with their weapons of bows and arrows, and found total pride that their mortality in any battle was very low.[60] It is a reality that some native tribes did enjoy the act of warfare. Walter Goldschmidt and Harold Driver, of American Archaeology and Ethnology out of U.C. Berkeley and Los Angeles has mentioned,

---

60 Miller, Virginia P. "Yuki of Northern California." In *Encyclopedia of Genocide and Crimes Against Humanity*, edited by Dinah L. Shelton, 1177-1179. Vol. 3. Detroit, MI: Macmillan Reference USA, 2005. *Global Issues in Context* (accessed April 6, 2019). http://link.galegroup.com.ezproxy.snhu.edu/apps/doc/CX3434600372/GIC?u=nhc_main&sid=GIC&xid=410ccd53.

"The most important is the adherence of prestige to certain objects of wealth-a concept that is considered to be characteristic of the entire Northwest Coast culture area. The chief desire of any normal male tribe member was the possession of these objects, and this standard of values had a marked effect on his daily life as well as on his very personality. Wealth is definitely a correlate with social position and is more than a mere symbol of social distinctions, for in a society where its acquisition is a major social drive,' where wealth buys specific privileges, it is an actual source of power and social status." [61]

A first-hand account from Hinton R. Helper helps further describe the local native peoples in his experiences in northern California,. Mr. Helper was an abolitionist author, lecturer and also diplomat to Argentina for the United States. He visited northern California in 1855, and wrote of his specific observations of the local natives, their diets and liberal gambling obsession:

"OF all the aborigines that are known to travelers within the limits of the western continent, the Digger Indians are certainly the most filthy and abominable. A worse set of vagabonds cannot be found bearing the human form. They come into the world and go from it to as little purpose as other carnivorous animals. Their chief characteristics are indolence and gluttony.

---

[61] Goldschmidt, Walter R., and Harold E. Driver. "The Hupa: White Deerskin Dance." *University of California Publications in American Archeology and Ethnology* 35, no. 8 (1940), 107-108.

"Partially wrapped in filthy rags, with their persons unwashed, hair uncombed and swarming with vermin, they may be seen loitering about the kitchens and slaughter-houses awaiting with eager gaze to seize upon and devour like hungry wolves such offal or garbage as may be thrown to them from time to time. Grasshoppers, snails and wasps are favorite delicacies with them, and they have a peculiar relish for a certain little animal, which the Bible tells us greatly afflicted the Egyptians in the days of Pharaoh."

"The male Digger never hunts—he is too lazy for this; he usually depends upon the exertions of his squaw to provide something or other to satisfy the cravings of hunger.

"The term Digger has been applied to these Indians in consequence of their method of procuring their food. The grasshopper or cricket of California is one of their favorite messes. They capture these insects by first digging a pit in the ground, and then forming a wide circle round it which is gradually narrowed. In this manner they drive the insects to the pit and there capture them. After having secured their prey, the next thing is to prepare it for food. This is accomplished either by baking the grasshoppers in the fire or drying them in the sun, after which the Diggers pulverize them.

"The epicures among them crush service-berries into a jam and thoroughly incorporate the pulverized insects with the pulpy mass to which they have reduced the fruit. Others mix their cricket meal with parched sunflower seed, but this is an advance in civilization and in the luxuries of the table, which is made by very few of them. They obtain the young wasps by burning the grass, which exposes the nests and enables them to grub in the earth for this delicacy.

"Acorns are also a favorite article of diet with these wretched creatures. In California, this fruit is larger and more palatable than with us, and it has the merit of being a cleaner kind of food than that which usually satisfies the Digger's hunger. Rude as these people are, they have sense enough to observe that all years are not equally productive in these nuts, and foresight sufficient to lay in a good stock during the plentiful years. (...)

"These Indians are inveterate gamblers, and when they have been so fortunate as to obtain clothing, they are almost sure to gamble it away before they stop. Their game is carried on as follows. A number sit cross-legged on the ground in a circle, and they are then divided into two parties, each of which has two head players. A ball is passed rapidly from hand to hand along the whole of one party, while the other attempts to guess in what hand it is. If successful, it counts one for the guessing party towards the game. If unsuccessful, it counts one in favor of the opposite party.

"The count is kept with sticks. All the while this is going on, they grunt in chorus, swinging their bodies to keep time with their grunts. The articles staked are placed in the centre of the ring. When they once get excited in play, they never stop so long as they have anything to stake. After getting through with their money, their trinkets and their provisions, they stake their clothes and keep on gambling till they reduce themselves to the costume of Adam."

"They are too indolent to work, too cowardly to fight. When pinched by the severity of hunger, and unable to procure their customary filthy diet, they are driven to the settlements, where they steal if they can, and do a little labor if they must. No sooner, however, have they procured the means of satisfying their immediate wants, than they abandon the employment offered them and relapse into their customary indolent habits."[62]

There has always been a stigma that material, or physical possessions, are something that is not perceived by the native cultures. This is a fallacy in the case of tribal native culture as you read above. So essentially wealth truly does plays a key component in the lifestyles of the indigenous cultures of the region. Acquisition of wealth is a major social drive to native tribes, and these tribes tended to exhibit a war-like demeaner to outsiders because of this legitimate way-of-life. Individual wealth in the tribe equals power and is even more justified by legal codes.

California tribal researchers Goldschmidt and Driver explain:

"That wealth is actual power is shown more clearly by the local tribal legal code. There is no vested authority or tribunal; atonement for any infraction of justice is

---

[62] Helper, Hinton R. "The Land of Gold. Reality Versus Fiction." The Library of Congress. Accessed April 22, 2019. http://www.loc.gov/resource/calbk.075. pp. 144-147.

brought about at the instigation of the offended party or his family. There is no crime against the society, only against other members of the society. Settlements following acts of violence or insults are handled by a go-between. The native is quick to take offense at an insult as well as to take action for a major crime, and his demand is always expressed in terms of money or native wealth. Though theoretically every infraction of justice has its set price in native goods, actually a man demands as much as he can according to his status in the society."[63]

Ultimately, as in every society, there is a leader and the rest fall underneath. There are community codes and rules to follow (laws) and in tribal societies like the Hupa, material wealth is actual power within the tribe itself. Native American criminal justice during these times could be paralleled to being just as draconian as those punishments served up in the early-European colonial period. Even further. The middle east. With a formal system set by community codes and guidelines, even the native tribes of Northern California had a legal system – as all formal communities do. To blindly accept the notion that all natives were peaceful and willing to coexist is a complete fallacy.

All communities since the beginning of time have always had rebels and law breakers. In all societies, no matter how big or small, community justice is something essential to any human civilization. There are always

---

[63] Ibid., Goldschmidt and Driver. p. 109.

rules to be held, until only recently, humans have all held themselves accountable to a higher divinity. It is through this, that law is an organic part of human nature regardless of culture or religion. Believe it or not—even the indigenous natives of Northern California (as with all world cultures) have some basic form of criminal justice based off of religious principles.[64] This is done in one form or another.

---

64 Fichtelberg, Aaron. "Chapter 3 - International Criminal Justice." In *Crime Without Borders: An Introduction to International Criminal Justice*, p. 33. Upper Saddle River: Prentice Hall, 2008.

FAILURES OF RESTRAINT

Enforcing any new, or already established laws on the wild western frontier was clearly a rough task for the U.S. Government, let alone the small local communities of hard-digging miners. In the late-1840's, poverty stricken individuals left all familiar structures behind, and were free to embody a new personality built into their journey for wealth and other new life experiences. These newly constituted communities had to find ways to deal with the increased recklessness on the trails they used for logistics, which meant instituting a popular judicial system.[65] This was truly an old wild west way of criminal justice.

A "president" and a jury were elected from amongst the community of miners. The most common penalty for theft, particularly in those days of gold fever, was a punctual death by hanging. Even Edward Hotchkiss, a visiting merchant from New England in 1850, spent over a year and a half in both Sacramento and San Francisco. He saw the societal issues firsthand. On June 9th, Mr.

---

65 Dame Shirley, *California in 1851[-1852]*; *the letters of Dame Shirley*, (San Francisco: The Grabhorn Press, 1933), p. 122

Hotchkiss wrote his mother of his personal experiences in San Francisco. He mentioned he found that Sundays were desecrated in the city. There were moral vices causing extreme social issues within the newly established timber and mining communities of Northern California, such as "gambling and other sorry activities."[66]

These vices were enabled by the lawlessness of the new territory and continued to facilitate it's way throughout California's short wild west history. As we see here, morals and ethics were a foundational issue facing the lawlessness of the "unprincipled" American settlers. One of the earliest settlers to the Humboldt Bay area was a man by the name of Bernardo Nordheimer. In his log entries during his early travels it was mentioned that, "death from accidents or from an occasional Indian attack seemingly was around every turn on a trail or bend in a river or stream."[67]

Incidental enough, in May of 1850, Mr. Van Duzen of Mr. Griggs party (one of the originals to land in Humboldt Bay) was exploring the area of Klamath when his pack-train of animals were attacked and butchered by local tribal natives.[68] While no civilians or military personnel became casualties of this attack, it certainly gave

---

66 "The California Letters of Edward Hotchkiss," in *California Historical Society Quarterly*, XII (June, 1933), p. 106.
67 See George Gibbs' Journal, Astoria, Oregon, Oregon Territory, 1850-1853, Smithsonian Archives, Capital Gallery Building, Washington D.C. "5, 6, 7." (note: journal pages were unnumbered.)
68 *Ibid.*

the settlers an unwelcome feeling to the area... at least once news got out. John W. Whaley, American settler and party leader, reached Humboldt Bay on June 22nd 1850.

His goal was to travel north by land, to assist in settling the bay. During the journey by land from San Francisco, Whaley observed numerous natives living around the shoreline. He would also record that Humboldt natives stole his cattle being driven in by members of his settling party. The local natives of the area would again come to show the newly arrived settlers that they truly were not welcome to settle Humboldt Bay.[69] The pioneer settlers of Northern California had been having continuous conflict with the Indians who were hostile to the American newcomers settling on native territory.

On January 10, 1856, the citizens of Crescent City located in Klamath County, desired to have military protection. They petitioned Governor J. Neely Johnson for his assistance and asked for a volunteer company to be supplied with the necessary firearms and ammunition. It was time to request drastic change in the U.S. government's policy of authority and it's guaranteed protection for the citizens of Northern California and for the residents of the local communities.

Following is the citizen petition to the State of California in 1856:

To his Excellency J. Neely Johnson, Governor of the State of California,

---

69 *Ibid.* 5.

We the undersigned petitioners, do most respectfully urge upon your Excellency's consideration, the dangerous and alarming position of many of the inhabitants of the northern portion of the State, and more particularly those of the County of Klamath, in the vicinity of Crescent City,

And for the benefit and general safety of fellow citizens in that portion of the State from the aggression of the numerous hostile Indians, from whom they have already suffered so much, and who are at the present time at open warfare with our citizens; We therefore respectfully urge upon your Excellency the necessity of giving them some immediate and prompt relief, and for that purpose respectfully petition your Excellency to call out in the service of the State, one volunteer company. Knowing the same to be necessary for the protection of the lives and property of its inhabitants.

Hoping your Excellency will give this appeal the prompt and decided action the necessity of the case demands,

We have the honor to subscribe ourselves your Excellency's most obt. svts.

(Signed)
I. D. Bosh - Walter McDonald - A. G. Whipple - C. A. Hillman - L. D. Watkins - Sacramento City January 10, 1856[70]

---

[70] Original on tile State Archives California State Capitol. Photostatic copy on file Adjutant General's Office (1856).

About a week later Governor Johnson gave the citizen petition to the Senate and Assembly. At the time they were actually in session with the following communication:

Executive Department January 15, 1856

To the Hon: The Senate and Assembly of the State of California;

I herewith present a communication in relation to Indian disturbances, in the northern portion of this State, signed by the Honorables J. D. Cosby, and Walter McDonald, besides by otherwell known citizens.

It will be seen that the signers of such petition request the aid of one volunteer company for the protection of the citizens against hostile Indians; but deeming the authority of the Executive, to accede to such request, under existing circumstances, at least a matter of doubtful propriety, I would therefore respectfully call your immediate attention to this subject., that you may take such action herein, as a due regard for the best interests of the State, and the protection of her citizens demand, at the hands of the Government. – I would also inform your Hon. Bodies that my predecessor in office on the 19th Inst. issued an order directing thirty men, to be called into the service of the State for the purposes indicated in the petition herein referred to. 'The only information known., on which this statement is founded is derived from a memorandum to that effect in the order Book of the Sect. of State, and I am therefore unable to furnish any additional information as to the action, if any, taken in pursuance of such order.

I have the honor to be - Very respectfully,
Your obt. svt. - (signed)
J. Neely Johnson - Governor[71]

---

[71] Original California State Archives., State Capitol. Photostatic copy Adjutant General's Office (1856).

THE GOVENOR & THE MILITIA

It's not a wonder that most American settlers in northern California felt that the natives were the aggressors. This problem would compound when the natives resisted attempts to undermine the United States government and their rights to traditional or treaty-given land rights. George Crook was the commanding officer while at Fort Jones, California, 1853. He mentioned, "Good faith forms no part of the Indian's nature." This was typical of local opinion at the time. The region at that time had little influence politically, and very rural. The world-renowned giant redwood forests were a central location to much of the hostility and underhandedness that had taken place between settlers and the natives.

In the decade between 1850 and 1860, the government of California would spend three million dollars in tax money to alleviate the depredation issue. The United States Army in California had issues in penetrating the terrain and its difficult tasks of finding an "invisible enemy." Seemingly impassable mountains, wide streams and entangled undergrowth, would give complete understanding to the comment: "It should be so difficult a matter to bring to justice a few score of savages, rendering the rapid and certain movements of troops a matter of difficulty and affording innumerable hiding places to the enemy," explained one U.S. Army official in northern California.

Extracted from Early California Laws and Policies Related to California Indians, Kimberly Johnston-Dodds, of the California Research Bureau writes:

"Article VII of the first California Constitution gave the Governor the power "to call for the militia, to execute the laws of the State, to suppress insurrections, and repel invasions." In his annual address to the California Legislature on January 7, 1851, Governor Burnett highlighted significant events that transpired during 1850, including "repeated calls...upon the Executive for the aid of the militia to resist and punish the attacks of the Indians upon the frontier." During 1850, Governor Burnett called out the militia two times.

"The first order was prompted by incidents at the confluence of the Gila and Colorado rivers on April 23, 1850; in response, the Governor ordered the sheriffs of San Diego and Los Angeles to organize a total of 100 men to "pursue such energetic measures to punish the Indians, bring them to terms, and protect the emigrants on their way to California." The second instance occurred in October 1850, when Governor Burnett ordered the sheriff of El Dorado County to muster 200 men. The commanders were instructed to "proceed to punish the Indians engaged in the late attacks in the vicinity of

Ringgold, and along the emigrant trail leading from Salt Lake to California."[72]

Governor Burnett explained calling out the militia as follows:

"In these cases the [Indian] attacks were far more formidable, and made at point where the two great emigrant trails enter the State...occurred at a period when the emigrants were arriving across the plains with their jaded and broken down animals, and them destitute of provisions. Under these circumstances, I deemed it due to humanity, and to our brethren arriving among us in a condition so helpless, to afford them all the protection within the power of the State..."

Had it been once known to our fellow citizens east of the Rocky Mountains, that the Indians were most hostile and formidable on the latter and more difficult portion of the route...and that the State of California would render no assistance to parties so destitute, the emigration of families to the State across the plains would have been greatly interrupted and retarded."

Mrs. Johnston-Dodds continues:

"From 1997 to 1999, the Sacramento Genealogical Society researched and compiled an extensive index of the State Militia Muster Rolls located in the California State Archives. The California State Archives contain Muster Rolls or organizational documents for 303 units

---

[72] "California Militia and Expeditions Against the Indians, 1850 - 1859." The California State Military Museum. Accessed April 25, 2019. http://militarymuseum.org/MilitiaandIndians.html.

located in most California counties. Seventy-one of the militias were located in San Francisco. After exhaustive review and crosschecking of 70,000 registered names, the researchers determined that approximately 35,000 men were listed on the Muster Rolls (attendance records). Muster Rolls may exist in other county or local archival repositories. The California State Archives does not have Muster Rolls for Colusa, Fresno, Glenn, Imperial, Inyo, Kern, Kings, Lake, Madera, Mendocino, Merced, Modoc, Riverside, San Benito, and Ventura counties for the period 1851 to 1866."[73]

"In April 1850, the California Legislature enacted two laws: An Act concerning Volunteer or Independent Companies, and An Act concerning the organization of the Militia. The Volunteer Act provided that citizens of any one county could:

- organize into a volunteer or independent company;
- arm and equip themselves in the same manner as the army of the United States;
- prepare muster rolls (attendance records) twice a year; and
- render prompt assistance and full obedience when summoned or commanded under the law.

"The lengthy Militia Act established in great detail the organization, ranks, rules, duties and commutation

---

73 *Ibid.*

fees (fees in lieu of service) that governed state military service. All "free, white, able-bodied male citizens, between the ages of eighteen and forty-five years, residing in [the] State" were subject to state-mandated military duty. Important provisions relating to the delegation of authority to command and call out troops provided that:

- the Governor was the commander in chief of all the forces in the state;
- the Legislature elected four Major Generals, eight Brigadier Generals, one Adjutant General and Quarter Master General (with Brigadier General rank);
- the Governor commissioned all of the officers under the Act, who then took the oath of office prescribed by the California Constitution;
- the State Treasurer initially was the ex officio Pay Master; and
- upon the Governor's orders, the Sheriffs of each county were responsible to call the enrolled militia.

Mr. Lamar was the Minority Leader of the Special Joint Committee in Congress who had stated, "the testimony will disclose the guilty parties, and from the just indignation of outraged humanity I have no desire to screen them; but for the mass of citizens engaged in this Indian warfare, I claim that they have acted from the strongest motives that govern human action, the defense of life and property."[74] A "Special Joint Committee" is a group of political individuals from U.S. Congress, who's job is to emphasis into the investigation of specific political outcomings. For example a headline report in the newspaper of domestic espionage effecting a national interests abroad, would spark an investigation by a "Special Joint Committee."

FINANCIAL EXPENDETURES BY CALIFORNIA STATE

Table 1: "General Recapitulation of the Expenditures incurred by the State of California For the Subsistence and Pay of the Troops, composing of the different Military Expeditions, ordered out by the Governor, during the Years 1850, 1851 and 1852, For the Protection of the Lives and Property of her Citizens, and for the Suppression of Indian Hostilities within her Borders."

Expeditions Against the Natives	Amount
Mariposa and Monterey	$259, 372.31
First El Dorado	101,861.65
Second El Dorado	199,784.59
Los Angeles and Utah	96,184.60

---

[74] "Minority Report of the Special Joint Committee on the Mendocino War," in Appendix to Journals of the Senate, of the Eleventh Session of the Legislature of the State of California, (Sacramento: C.T. Botts, State Printer, 1860), 10.

Trinity, Klamath and Clear Lake	34,320.08
San Diego "Fitzgerald Volunteers"	22,581.00
Siskiyou "Volunteer Rangers"	14,987.00
Gila "Colorado Volunteers"	113,482.25
Amount paid in War Bonds by Paymasters	1,000.00
Total Amount	$843,573.48

Source: Comptroller of the State of California, Expenditures for Military Expeditions Against Indians, 1851-1859, (Sacramento: The Comptroller), Secretary of State, California State Archives, Located at "Roster" Comptroller No. 574, Vault, Bin 393.

Table 2: California State's expenditures for expeditions from 1854 to 1859.

Expeditions Named in the "Act of Appropriations" by Congress were made on March 2, 1861

Expedition	Year	Amount Allowed by California*	Amount Allowed by United States**	Amount Disallowed by United States
Shasta Expedition	1854	4,068.64	1,261.38	2,807.26
Siskiyou Expedition	1855	14,036.36	6,146.60	7,889.76
Klamath & Humboldt Expedition	1855	99,096.65	61,537.48	37,559.17
San Bernardino Expedition	1855	817.03	419.99	397.04

Klamath Expedition	1856	6,190.07	2953.77	3,237.30
Modoc Expedition	1856	188,324.22	80,436.72	107,887.50
Tulare Expedition	1856	12,732.23	3,647.25	9,084.98
Klamath & Humboldt Expedition	1858/1859	52,184.45	31,823.94	20,360.51
Pitt River Expedition	1859	72,156.09	41,761.54	30,394.55
Total		$449,605.74	$229,987.67	$219,618.07

Source: Comptroller of the State of California, Expenditures for Military Expeditions Against Indians, 1851-1859, (Sacramento: The Comptroller), Secretary of State, California State Archives, Located at "Roster" Comptroller No. 574, Vault, Bin 393.
*Amount submitted to the United States for reimbursement.
**Amount actually paid by the United States.

Local militias had the distinction of been formed by a special act of legislature, March 12, 1856. Crescent City is located on the coast in Klamath County, and was in continuous danger from the hostile native tribes in the region. They began to protect the residents of the county by forming a military company. The Klamath Mounted Rangers were organized on April 27, 1854, and had sixty-six men on the roster. W. J. Terry took command as Captain, leading the volunteer unit into and outside of the county.

Many of the hostile encounters carried on against the natives were typically in densely forested areas and because many members of this company were expert trackers, they were of excellent use. W.J. Terry's militia unit and his ability to lead was noted for his "ability to push on in spite of every obstacle thrown in the way by the enemy." [75] The volunteers would further experienced a lot of fighting when the unit in company with the Union (Arcata) volunteer's, took the field against the natives of the Tule Lake Region, in a short but bloody campaign.

Later, the Klamath Rangers went up against some hostile tribal elements on Smith River which resulted in the death of five natives. This combat was in retaliation for attacks made upon the local citizenry by the Indians.[76] Although there is no further record of activities of this company, it is evident from the few items available, that the Klamath Mounted Rangers' activities to halt Indian depredations, were effective for the time being. The Adjutant General's Report for April 1861 stated the volunteer company had been organized during the "Indian hostilities, and was now disbanded."

The above example shows the general process of the organization of many of the early militia companies. "First, the people's petition for protection; second, the Governor's aid to the people by presenting the petition to the Legislative bodies for their authority in providing

---

75 *Sacramento Union*, October 30, 1855, page 2, column 2
76 *Sacramento Union*, January 19, 1855, page 2, column 1

the necessary funds and third, formal-passage of the Legislative Act to give the proper legality for the procedure of organizing the company." [77] These companies were organized for the purposes of policing local native depredations committed in the region. This was the only way for the citizens of the region to defend their families and themselves.

"Two young men by the name of Cooper were living on Eel River, going out to meet a sick brother who was coming in on the trail from the Trinity early in November were killed by the Indians on Yager Creek, running into S. fork of Trinity. The murder was known among the Klamath Indians before the news reached their friends. One of their hats being found, a party went out from Eel river & found their bodies much mutilated... The murder of the Negro on Bald Hills during the past summer was traced to the Lagoon Indians near Trinidad. An Indian of the Trinity living at the ferry offered to take the Whites at once to the place & point out the murderer."[78]

The preceding quote is a description of how the Tompkins Ferry massacre began. First, with the pre-meditated murder of a man named "Bender" who was a "packer." The local natives would also end up killing Mr. Blackburn, or "elder Blackburn." In this account, it appears that this massacre was a senseless act of violence that

---

[77] "Citizens of Crescent City." The California State Military Museum: Welcome to California Military History Online!. Last modified August 10, 2017. http://militarymuseum.org/CrescentCity.html.
[78] *Ibid.* 10, 11.

served the interest of nobody. The local natives would soon after also end up killing three more settlers by the surnames of "Skink, Cushing and Walker." Murders also deemed unwarranted:

"The ferry house consisted of a cloth house or large tent in front of a small clapboard building. In the former were three men. In the latter the younger Blackburn & his wife slept. Early in the morning the Indians cut open the Sail house and killed the three men. A noise one of them made awakened Blackburn who went to the door where an Indian jumped at him and he had just time to get back and bolt the door. They then commenced hurling stones to break in the house and attempted to fire it. Blackburn had two guns and his wife loaded for him to fire. he fired 20 rounds and as was believed killed 7 Indians."

"Two of them came with a brand swinging it. One he shot when the other took it up and he killed him also. This struck them with a panic and they drew back. About 8 o'clock they hauled off. The squaws [?'tried'] to get his wife by telling her that it was all quiet. About 10 A.M. a pack train came up and relieved them. The Indians expressed great admiration of the conduct of the woman. It is difficult to tell what was the real motive of the act. It is generally alleged to have arisen from the conduct of a boy who had made a practice of insulting the women."[79]

Although it was unprincipled behavior by a young settler boy that instigated the tensions, the native

---

79   *ibid.* 12.

response was completely unwarranted. Like most of the local settlers organic responses to the indigenous attacks, a volunteer militia was raised to find the guilty natives responsible for the murders. The militia would eventually return empty handed, despite the fact that a Trinity native had a pistol that would belong to Mr. Walker of the deceased. However, upon returning back to Trinidad, the body of Dr. Higgenbottom in a gulch leading into Redwood Creek.

It seems that the bodies of American settlers were turning up quite often, but to the extreme frustrations of the communities, few natives were found to be responsible for the crimes. More and more reports came in of community members and settlers being murdered at the hands of Northern California's natives. Rage inflamed the settling communities and they would demand government intervention. However, as the demand would not effectively be met, in keeping to their constitutional rights formed volunteer militias to defend themselves and take the law into their own hands. It's not a wonder that the volunteer militia units would end up killing native warriors in retaliation without regard to guilt or innocence.

In the Klamath natives lodges, a private basket for each man in the tribe is maintained and stored in the lodge house; a communal-political building for the tribal community. Within this private basket is the personal records of each man. Most notably two records in particular stood out: "the men they have killed by a red mark." – of course as aforementioned, some Northern California tribes took absolute pride in warfare. The other, "The number of their wives by a black one."[80] Outside of warfare, tribal warriors would partake in gambling. One example is a game called "toop-stick." The losing gambler is banished from tribal lands for a handful of days with just a flint and will bathe themselves.

Some local natives treated their tribal squaws (women) as polygamists, some had open relationships, and sometimes they just replaced wives after a deathly illness.[81] After death, in a ceremony, this private basket is placed in a woven case and hidden in the hollow of a tree on a hill overlooking the village. If the warrior owned a canoe, they would break it apart and place the pieces over his grave. Even more, the men of the tribes have tattoos to some extent. They also marked the number of enemies killed by scars on the chest.[82] This type of symbolism shows the warlike disposition and character some of the native tribes of Northern California towards warfare, honor, and ceremony.

---

80 *Ibid.* 13, these passages are titled "Driscell" and "Wm. N. Bercaw."
81 Hurtado, Albert L. ""Hardly a Farm House--A Kitchen without Them": Indian and White Households on the California Borderland Frontier in 1860." *The Western Historical Quarterly*13, no. 3 (1982): p. 256. doi:10.2307/969413.
82 *Ibid.* 13.

DEPREDATIONS

The American settlers who came to Northern California, were not dealing with the typical issues of days past. As time increased, problems did as well. A snowball-effect as it were. Social problems and tensional conflict between the settlers and natives began to spiral out of control. On the South Fork of the Eel River, two brothers by the names of Atwood and Gilbert Sproul were clearing land of brush and thicket off of the river's edge. The Sproul brothers were excitedly building a farm for future crops, like their neighbor directly across the riverbank who settled a homestead by the last name of Armstrong. Later that afternoon, a band of local natives surprise attacked the brothers out of nowhere. Ultimately, the Sproul brothers would end up receiving serious injuries in the attack while successfully defending their house.[83]

The American settlers of the Northern California region felt an unusual severity to the events that had transcended upon the area in the mid-1800's. After a

---

83 Bledsoe, Anthony J. *Indian Wars of the Northwest: A California Sketch.* San Francisco : Bacon & Company, 1885.

handful of years of feuding between the settlers and natives; the indigenous tribes were now shamelessly bold, restless, and vengeful. The rumors of a war between the native tribes of the valleys and mountains reached a zenith. Cattle-farmers living in the higher elevations completely abandoned their homes, and planters even abandoned their farm plows which were left eroding in the elements. There were healthy fears rumoring about war paths involving roving bands of natives that were active in an effort to purge the region of its incoming settler population.

The following is a journal entry about the first-hand account of the murders of the Hickock children at the hands of local natives:

"In the settlement of Butte, Tehama and Shasta counties in the early sixties the people living in and along the foot hills were in danger of being slain by a band of Indians, known as the Mill Creeks as their main camp was at Black Rock on Mill Creek. They were a cruel, bloodthirsty band. The chief was called Big Foot, as he had six toes on his right foot.

"The killing of the Hickok children was in June, 1862. The Hickok children, two girls and a boy were gathering black berries on Rock Creek about three-quarters of a mile from their home when they were surrounded by a number of Indians. They first shot the oldest girl, she was seventeen years old. When found she was entirely nude. They then shot the younger girl, fifteen years old, but she ran to Rock Creek and fell with her face in the water.

"They did not take her clothing as she was in full dress when found. Just then Tom Allen came upon the scene. He was hauling lumber for a man by the name of Keefer. They immediately attacked Allen. He was found scalped with his throat cut. Seventeen arrows had been shot in him and seven had gone partly through so that they had to be pulled out the opposite side.

"The little boy of twelve years, they captured and took with them. A company of about thirty men started after the Indians. They did not know anything about tracking the Indians and went in the hills without provisions and had to come back. This Mr. Keefer had a rancheria on his ranch, a sawmill in the mountains and a grist mill a short distance below the Hickok home. Mr. Keefer sent for Hi. Good, who was known to be a great Indian trailer, and Indian fighter. When Good arrived Mr. Keefer said, "Mr. Good, I want you to get the Hickok boy, you can have all the money you want." He then emptied his purse of seventy-five dollars and gave it to Good.

"Good had a man living with him by the name of Bowman, so he and Bowman, William Sublet and Obe Fields went to the Indian camp at Black Rock, which they found deserted. The finally found the trail going north out of the canyon. This they followed up a long ridge and near the top they found the boy by the odor. They made a litter of their clothing and packed the little fellow out to Good's place in the valley, thirty-five miles. It was a trip that none but heroic men could endure. The little boy was buried by the side of his sisters in the Chico cemetery.

"My wife went to school with the baby sister of the Hickok children. She used to cry and tell about the massacre.

"The first person buried in the Chico cemetery was a man by the name of Fry, he was killed by the Mill Creek Indians. T. F. Rinehart provided in his will for a monument to be put at Fry's grave."[84]

The local residents in Northern California's settlements and towns would begin to wonder how it is that the natives would come to acquire weapons and ammunition so easily. Unprincipled settlers would end up enabling hostilities through local arms trade with the natives of the area. Knowingly or not, these trade deals would both benefit and have consequential results for both parties. These handfuls of settlers would end up teaching them some tricks to be resourceful as well. For instance, melting tea-pots for ammunition.

The Marysville Daily Herald published "How the Indians Get Their Lead." In it, the author makes reference to how the native squaws would transit town collecting old tea caddies. The natives would end up melting down up to 50 pounds of lead daily from unknown sources. They would use this lead in furnishing firearms. The editor of this article also stated that the people engaged in dealing with the natives may not want to show their face

---

84 "The Last of the Mill Creeks, and Early Life in Northern California,." The Library of Congress. Accessed April 21, 2019. http://www.loc.gov/resource/calbk.173.

in town again.[85] The local tribes were very resourceful and preparing well for warfare.

A refugee status of sorts began to happen within the area, with mountain settlers arriving into the larger cities. Community members began looking to take precautions from this impending outbreak of hostilities, immediately reached out to community officials for protection. A convention was held, and legal communication was signed by many local citizens to Humboldt Bay. In this article, the citizens stated that "they were of the firm belief that the bay Indians should be kept on the Klamath Reservation, and recommending their immediate removal."[86] The citizens of Hydesville sent a similar communication to the areas authorities as well.

The citizens of the area were not dealing with normal social problems. The little bit of peace that was being felt by the Humboldt Bay residents were now all but gone, and the hostile tensions rapidly constricted around them. In the fall of 1860, a couple of Humboldt Bay settlers had their cattle stampeded off of their property by a band of ten hostile natives. Two days after the property crime had occurred, a party of seven settlers (presumably neighbors of the property loss victims) followed the trail of the retreating natives for about twenty-four hours non-stop. At approximately 4pm, the party of natives

---

85 "How the Indians Get Their Lead." *Marysville Daily Herald.* 21 November 1855, col. page 2, col. 3.
86 *Ibid.* p. 332.

were discovered in a ravine with a large portion of their fellow tribe.

The volunteer militia openly charged the group after one opening shot from a pistol. After a brief melee, thirteen natives were killed. A couple would escape severely wounded, unknowing if they had survived. The natives rancheria was punctually sacked and razed. Not surprisingly, articles of settlers personal property and provisions were recovered from that same rancheria. This retaliatory incident is an illustration and example of what had certainly built up on already poor and hostile settler/native relations.

John Fulwider, a foothill resident, had his house robbed in February, which drove him from his house. Mr. Larabee of the same neighborhood, was found murdered. His cattle and homestead razed to the ground by local natives. Ann Quinn, who was Mr. Larabee's cook at his ranch, was murdered and purposely burned in the building. The attack on Mr. Larabee's ranch was all too audible. Neighborhood resident David King was plowing his farm near his homestead.

He heard the commotion, picked up his rifle and began to run towards the uproar. He was ill-prepared, as the natives used firearms and forced Mr. King to flee the scene. It is documented that Mr. Fulwider was assumed dead, as no body was recovered. However, his favorite hat was found on the bank of the Mad River. There had one bullet-hole in the lower half of the hat; soaked in blood.[87] Of course, this is just another illustration on one of many other outrages that happened as time passed on.

In the Spring of 1861, there was a discovery of a plot among the natives to exterminate the entire settler population of the Hupa Valley. It was a seeming exodus from the area. Settlers entire families packed their homes to flee. Other settlers homes were fortified and sealed with heavy barriers to defend their private property and livelihoods. The settlers excitement to this news was in part to the credibility of the intelligence known.

Surprisingly, the Hupa tribe for the last decade was one of the more peaceful of any of the tribes in the Northern California region. So, for the settlers, it was almost unbelievable that these rumors of intrigue and hostile intentions would be taken for truth. Sadly, the fact became known beyond any dispute that the regional tribes of Northern California were actually scheming to massacre the entire settlement population. The truth is – the native tribes of the local region were secretly preparing for open warfare and hostilities on all American settlers.

During early Spring, two citizen residents by the name of John Brehmer and A. W. Turner had recently lost a lot of private property to local native attacks. The two men received support from the U.S. Army at Fort Humboldt, located just above Bucksport outside Eureka. Five soldiers and five volunteers tracked the thieves

---

87   *Ibid.* p. 333

to Boulder Creek, located about seven miles from Blue Slide just off of the Mad River. The recovering party assaulted the natives when coming onto their rancheria. There were thirty-four native casualties, with 14 being killed. On the rancheria, several hundred pounds of fresh beef, clothing, and many household goods were recovered. This was all property that had been stolen from the areas settlers.

The natives of the region were moving constantly. At this point they were looking to perform surprise ambushes or avoid being attacked themselves. The U.S. Army, with its history of experience of fighting natives, knew that scouting at night would be best policy in preventing ambushes. This tactic would succeed, as a good number of natives, showing hostile motivations, were killed. The trails on the Trinity mountains which sit inland from the coast about 45 miles, and the only convenient logistical trail for provisions were constantly attacked by roving natives.

This would end up causing serious provision, food and financial issues for the settlers living on the coast. During one incident for example, the employees of Sanford & Company were making a camp when their pack-train was attacked by natives. Arrows rained on the packers, and one man by the name of Mr. Thompson took an arrow through his hand. The packers rebuked the attack and fortified their pack train with freight and saddles. The natives would continue their assault until reinforcements finally arrived, then fled.

Mr. Helper (the abolitionist author previously mentioned), would further mention in his journal about how a band of Klamath natives attempted to murder a pastor riding to Trinidad:

"In passing over the northern part of the district, it was impossible to reach the appoints without passing through the territory occupied by the Klamath tribe of Indians, who were considered among the most treacherous in all the northern part of the State, and the most dreaded by the whites, except it may be the bloody Modoc's, who murdered Dr. Thomas and George Canby.

These Indians had conceived a deadly dislike of Father Leahy, and had attempted to kill him by shooting at him as he was riding on horseback about two miles before reaching the little lumber camp called Trinidad. To escape, Brother Leahy had been compelled to take an open boat, leave his horse at Trinidad, and, sailing around the headlands of the bay, reach his home at Eureka."[88]

---

88 Helper, H. R. *Ibid.* p. 72.

A SERIOUS INACCURACY

November 7th 1861: "The contest between the whites and the Indians in Humboldt still goes on with unabated fury." Indians on Mad River kill and mutilate five farmers, "a terrible sight on this lonely prairie."[89] The volunteer militia's raised within the local communities of Northern California was a federal guarantee by way of Amendment II in the United States Constitution. "A well-regulated Militia, being necessary to the security of a free State, the right of the people to keep and bear Arms, shall not be infringed."[90] This personal right as an American citizen allows for the ability to join rank, or form a volunteer militia in times of domestic crisis. There are some historians and legal scholars that argue this constitutional right; however I believe this particular argument doesn't stand. So what is the argument then?

---

89 Roadarmel, Gordon C. "Some California Dates of 1861." *California Historical Society Quarterly* 39, no. 4. p. 357. (1960): 289-308. doi:10.2307/25155350.

90 Hamilton, Alexander, John Jay, and James Madison. "Constitution of the United States." In *The Federalist Papers*, p. 183. New York: Pocket Books, 1964.

The proposed, but fictional, opposing legal argument to this case is that neither the State of California, nor the Federal government sanctioned or approved of citizen militia operations against native depredations. It was ultimately the American government that finally attempted to step in to reign control over the native outbreak of hostilities. Still, this would prove to be a serious miscalculation by the politicians in California and Washington D.C. It was the dissolution of the volunteers that worked with U.S. Army regulars in the field that had dire consequences. The volunteer citizen experts served as guides in survival and tactics, on the mountains and over rough terrain. They also served as translators for native encounters. The disbanding of the volunteers is paralleled to fighting a war with one arm.

It was not a good situation for the settlers, or the Army. Starting in July of 1861, hostile native demonstrations began to occur daily in the areas of Kneeland, Big Bend, Redwood Creek, and Trinity. The U.S. Army, whose regular soldiers were stationed out of Fort Humboldt and Fort Gaston knew that they were under provisioned and extremely undermanned. The regular soldiers stationed in the "Far West" were regularly disenfranchised within their extremely rural and solitary confines, compared to that of their easterly stationed comrades. It was this primary lack of motivation that the U.S. regulars knew they could not fight the natives without the help and expertise of the citizen volunteers. Even worse... the local natives knew it. The native tribes of Northern California only feared the citizen volunteers.

When the rumors spread through pseudo-friendly valley tribes that the government barred volunteers from active service; the hostile mountain tribes began a campaign of complete terror that produced devastation and death in all directions. Further evidence of unbound hostile motivation proved itself when Jerry Wilson, a settler in the Union (Arcata) area suddenly went missing from the neighborhood. The search was on, but after two to three weeks of searching for Mr. Wilson, friends and neighbors organized to search for him. They believed he may have been killed or injured somehow; but instead found out through physical evidence to come to the conclusion that local natives had murdered him. Circumstantial evidence also pushed the understanding that he was first wounded and then dragged to an area hidden from view, then tortured to death.

George Gibbs, one of the founding members of Humboldt County, wrote in 1850:

"At Brehmer's Ranch, on Mad River, twenty miles from Union, were living Mr. Brehmer, John Stuart, Christian and Henry Lemke, brothers, and another man, who were engaged in herding cattle in the vicinity. On the morning of the 7th of November they left the house in search of cattle, each going in a different direction. Towards evening, as Henry Lemke was returning home, and while four or five miles from the house, he received a bullet in the back, which felled him from his horse in a senseless condition. When he returned to consciousness a minute later a number of hideous savages were stripping him of his clothes.

"Realizing that his only chance for life was to feign death, he succeeded by a powerful effort of the will in controlling his impulse to struggle with his assailants. He lay as limp and lifeless in their hands as though life had really left his body. They stripped him naked and started off; but one, as if to assure himself of the death of the victim, turned back and pointed a pistol at Lemke's head. The ball razed his neck, and burying itself in the ground threw dirt and gravel in his face. Still he lay motionless, exerting the full strength of his mind in a prodigious effort to refrain from every appearance of life. The ruse was successful. The Indians left him, and disappeared in the forest.

"Lemke rose to his feet and started on foot, naked, for Brehmer's house. He had gone but a little way when he saw his brother's horse, rider less, running toward him from an opposite direction. The horse knew him, and he caught and mounted the animal. When he reached the house it was vacant. None of the party who had gone out in the morning had returned. He turned away, and sick and faint, bleeding and dying, rode his brothers horse in the direction of the nearest neighbor's place, several miles distant. He met Brehmer and another man, who up to this time knew nothing of what had occurred. They returned to the house with Lemke, and through the night alternately guarded and watched over him. The wound he had received was mortal, and he died before morning. The next day the dead bodies of Christian Lemke and John Stuart were found on a trail near the house."[91]

Ultimately, there ended up being so many murders (many unaccounted for) throughout the new Northern California communities, that people outright chuckled at any idea of peace by that point. With rumors being confirmed as truth, the native tribes entered into a pact executing a plan to exterminate the "whites" or drive them from their homesteads and towns. Mass town-hall meetings were held for policy decisions on how to deal with the local natives; as well as securing their lives and personal property.

In the end, a community committee documented that "hostile tribes were continuing their depredations and showing an extraordinary malignity in their warfare, destroying property with savage wantonness, shooting settlers in the mountains and murdering citizens on the borders of the densest settlements." The committee was wholly represented by the local residents of the Humboldt settlements. If the residents felt obliged to protect themselves from the atrocities mentioned above, surely the committee would find approval naturally in their common defense.

The committee finalizes their statement, "... and whereas the Federal force was wholly insufficient to protect the lives of citizens ; therefore, the committee

---

[91] *Ibid.* 13. George Gibbs'.

recommended that resolutions be adopted that the Governor of the State be requested to ascertain whether the General commanding the Military Division of the Pacific was able and willing to send sufficient force to Humboldt county to secure peace and safety to the citizens. It was also resolved that the citizens request the Governor to authorize the enrollment of State troops."[92]

This document was immediately sent to the Governor of California. The second amendment in the U.S. constitution allows for volunteer militias to be formed in times of necessary protection and defense. The federal government could not provide that protection for the settlers of the Humboldt Bay area, and forming a citizen militia for physical enforcement would be the next appropriate way to solve a problem with a hostile foreign people. The right to "life & personal property" is a English common-law, and a Christian principle.[93] This is an attitude that would have been foreign to the tribal peoples of Northern California, as previously mentioned in an earlier chapter.

---

92 *Ibid*. 13. George Gibbs'.
93 Smith, Daniel L. *Our America: Our Life & Our Culture*. Print.. p. 46.

HOSTILITY IN UPPER CALIFORNIA

March, 1858. Governor Weller of California received a letter. In this letter was a declaration signed by the citizens of Union (Arcata), Humboldt County. This letter was received at his desk in Sacramento unexpectedly, and it reads:

"It has now been two months since the Indians in this vicinity started in open hostility to us, though so far they have confined their operations to the trail connecting this County to Weaverville. This being our direct channel of communication with the Sacramento Valley, and a trail over which the United States Mail must pass once a week, it is of the utmost importance that it should be kept open. The Indians on this trail first manifested their hostility to us by shooting a man who was traveling alone.

"We supposed that a few men would be sufficient to punish the Indians and make them ask for peace, and accordingly, a party was organized, provided for by private means and sent in search of the hostiles. After trailing the Indians for several days, they were attacked from ambush and one man was killed. In the meantime their camp which they had left unguarded was attacked, and ten mules were killed. This party consisted of only twelve men. Subsequently, another party of twenty-five men went out who were provisioned at a heavy private expense. In endeavoring to drive the Indians from the vicinity of the trails, they were fired upon in a deep canyon, and one man was killed, another wounded. The company has now disbanded, not feeling inclined to incur further danger and hardships at their own expense.

"The trails are now closed, there being no travel over them except by night or in large parties. The question now is what is- there to.be done? There are no troops here at the garrison and the people are not able to carry on a war at their own expense. The people of the county are of the opinion that if the militia could be called out, and arms furnished, the merchants would feel encouraged to furnish supplies, and wait for the State to pay. We can furnish the men if they can only be supplied."[94]

Governor Weller punctually responded by decreeing volunteer units to take up arms in Humboldt County for their own self-defense. Other cities, towns, and counties took up arms and formed volunteer militias to prosecute native attacks as well. With the American settlers under constant hostility from the local native tribes, and lack of government support, Governor Weller didn't have much of a choice – as citizens already had the legal right

---

94 "Humboldt Volunteers." The California State Military Museum. Accessed April 12, 2019. http://www.militarymuseum.org/HumboldtVolunteers.html.

to act on their own behalf. And – they promptly did so with authority.

On the Klamath trail, "...a train of mules... from Crescent City was attacked by the Indians; all the mules, together with the goods and provisions were taken off to the mountains in safety by the Indians; and everyone connected with the train was killed or carried off captive..."[95] An unofficial war between the settlers and natives of Northern California was going full speed. Both sides were looking to exterminate the other. Civilians and the little bits of civil authority in the settlements began to strategically hide women and children in places of known safety for fear of horrendous attacks.[96] The Daily National Democrat reported in August of 1858: "Several white men have lately been murdered by Indian between Humboldt and Yreka."

In the meantime, community residents near the same area, encountered a party of drunken local natives in early November of 1856. The count was 20 local natives, all of them male and female. They had with them a large handle of liquor; in which they consumed and became crazy and furious. They would then begin to fight with each other. After local civil authorities responded, three natives lie dead with their bodies badly disfigured. The

---

95 "More Indian Difficulties on the Klamath." *Marysville Herald,* 25 October 1855, col. 3 col. 1
96 "The Indian War." *Daily Evening Herald,* 26 August 1853, col. page 2, col. 2.

ones who did live were bleeding from many deep cuts and wounds.[97]

Further, two local native tribes would end up openly warring against each other near the town of Red Bluff in Tehama County. Even more, two settlers were killed in Deer Creek Valley in a random attack while farming, one of them by the name of Mr. Fillput.[98] The two warring parties were the Big Meadow and Mill Creek tribes. In the resulting war the natives had eight deaths, however, it was the most likely the safety concerns for the citizens of Red Bluff that would be of such worry to the locals.[99] Especially since a finely made volume of O.W. Holmes' (an American poet) poetry was recovered from this event. The situation was critical, as it was already on a downhill descent a few years prior:

The Marysville Herald would report:

"...not a day passes but some poor fellow falls a victim to Indian barbarity. The tribes in southern Oregon and northern California are joined in alliance to exterminate the white from the country. it is not safe for less than 10 men to venture beyond sight of their dwellings. The Indians fight with the desperation of despair... Those who have been accustomed to see the harmless and effeminate types of red men in middle California known little of those warlike tribes of the North. In them are...

---

[97] "Indian Fight." *Marysville Daily Herald,* 18 November 1856, col. page 2, col 2.(vol 7, no 91)

[98] "From Yreka." *Shasta Courier*, 16 June 1855, col. page 2, col. 2.

[99] "Indian Fight." *The Yreka Union,* 7 April 1866, col. page 3. (vol. 14, no. 25)

all dreaded qualities that characterize the Indians... They are bold, revengeful... they are no despicable foe in a war of extermination. the citizens... desire no interferences of the General Government to procure a peace. They are determined to leave not a vestige of the savage race alive."[100]

The residents of Yreka were about sick of the issues that the depredations that the local natives had been causing their community. "The lazy, lounging and miserable set of cowardly Indians that hang about this city and vicinity, are becoming an intolerable nuisance, almost causing enough indignations to make every person treat them as a set of highway robber and pirates." So what caused this public outcry in late-June, 1859? Indignations. This word is defined in this situation as hostile, and immoral.

A 14 year-old boy and his 10 year-old sister were riding home on horseback from the town of Yreka to the town of Table Rock. During their journey on a single horse, they were stopped and detained on the road by two local male natives. During the harassment, it was concluded that the natives were intending to buy or trade the girl in some way. At this point in desperation, on guarantee of freedom, the boy promised to bring them back a bottle of whiskey. The natives would not take this offer of alcohol for freedom. The two natives got busy

---

[100] "From the North." *Marysville Daily Herald,* 18 November 1855. col. page 2, col. 3.

rummaging through the children's clothing, which they just bought from Yreka.

The boy quickly switched the horse with his sister on its back! While the horse was galloping away, he yelled for his sister to "hang on tight!" One of the two natives opened fire from a gun one of them was brandishing, but missed. The boy ran away after the weapon discharged, and the two natives fled as well. Afterwards, the children punctually called on the authorities, and the posse was able to arrest to two natives after being positively identified by the children, as well as some Yreka locals. The citizens of Yreka would end up finalizing a statement in the local paper, "These evils must be put to an end in some peaceable manner, or the citizens near this city will be prompted to a summary punishment of these inhuman savages."[101]

In the evening of mid-October, a group natives attacked the house of Mr. Harris. A local tribesman who had been acting friendly to the local settlers walked into his house with a gun and shot him without a moment's notice. His ten-year old daughter was shot in the arm. Mrs. Harris continued to discharge her weapon at the natives and quickly reload. While the natives were kept at a distance, both Mrs. Harris and her daughter fled to hide in the bushes. The next morning, some mountain settlers arrived and rescued the two.[102]

---

101 *Ibid.*
102 "More About the Indian Difficulties in the North – Heroic Conduct of a Woman." *Marysville Herald,* 27 October 1855. col. 3 col 1).

Rumors of war. These were always an issue for the U.S. Army. When their charge is to protect American citizens and maintain the peace, prompt commitment could be slow in response. An editorial was published by the Red Bluff Beacon on June 19th, 1859 titled "More Cause." In the article, the citizens of the local communities are livid, "...the murder and other outrages published today should convince Governor Weller of the total inefficiency..."[103] They were speaking on the part of the governments inefficiency in acting on behalf of the citizens for protection of life and property and demanded immediate action.

---

103 "More Cause." *Red Bluff Beacon*, 29 June 1859. 2/1.

THE CONFLICT PEAKS

A couple was at home in the evening outside of Union (Arcata), when Redwood natives surprised them in a daring attack. Mrs. Weaver was killed with three guns beside her. Her male companion was abducted, and presumed dead.[104] Not too long after, three neighboring pig farmers by the names of Joeseph Bashow, Lewis Cash, and Mr. Mann were ambushed and executed. The trio were driving their hogs on a trail from Hydesville, when they needed to camp for the night to refresh from their tiring journey. What they didn't know was they were being tracked by local natives from the time they left their properties. When they crossed the Mad River, unaware, the trio was shot. Cattle drivers would later find the bodies of the farmers killed.[105]

The communities of the settling areas of Humboldt Bay were perpetually in mourning for their good and industrious citizens who were killed in their own houses. Some were killed on lonely trails, and in the woods. All

---
104 "Humboldt News." *Alta California,* 15 October 1862.
105 "Humboldt News." *Alta California,* 17 August 1863.

Daniel L. Smith

done at the hands of the hostile tribesmen. Residents would come to know this period in history as a "carnival of death," terrible to even contemplate the reality of the events.[106] In the Mattole region, a farmer living off of the Eel River by the name of O.W. Wise, was walking back towards his homestead one evening from his dairy shed housing the milk cows. While completely unaware of his situation, he was mortally wounded by six arrows and a rifle ball. He died the next day. Not more than a couple weeks after, an incident occurred to three settlers who were living in a house near the Van Duzen River.

On August 25th, Mr. Coates (one of the three men) was walking near his house when he was shot by a couple rifle rounds and killed from the brush. The other two roommates of Mr. Coates (who was unarmed), retrieved their rifles and attempted to protect him. One native was killed, out of the attacking party of twenty-five warriors. Eel River would remain a hotspot for hostile conflict for settlers and natives of the local area. The Humboldt Bay area was in the middle of what could be seen as blatant murder spree on the part of the natives against the settlers by these aforementioned accounts.[107]

The state of California and the United States government by this point had received the public outcry by the residents of Northern California. "Indians are still committing depredations, killing stock, robbing and

---

106 *Ibid.* "Some California Dates of 1861." (2)
107 *Ibid.* "Some California Dates of 1861." (3)

shooting at settlers."[108] Governor Johnson cooperated with U.S. Army General Wood to enlist the help of volunteers under the U.S. flag in support of appropriating significant sums of taxpayers money to overwhelm the native hostilities. Klamath county would be the starting off point of native suppression, with the financial backing of $515,000.00 in U.S. taxpayer funds.[109]

Fort Gaston, which sits right outside of Hupa Valley, was in a stir in early 1861. Captain Underwood, who was the Fort Commander at the time, found out that the Hupa tribe was in fact hostile and intent on committing to sieging the fort. The dilemma for Captain Underwood, was the fact that he had only 90 people available for its defense. There was intelligence of at least one-thousand Hupa warriors and allies ready for war within twenty miles of the fort.[110] Colonel Herbert M. Hart wrote of the inner-Humboldt depredations: "The intensity of operations did not reduce Indian depredations immediately. In July 1862, four settlers were attacked again while moving a herd to town. A recent patrol of soldiers arrived to find one body had been stripped of its clothes, the throat slashed, and the heart cut out."[111] The men's names Colonel Hart was talking about was William T.

---

108 "Later From Humboldt." *Alta California*, 7 August 1862.
109 "Appropriations for 1856 for Support of the Government." *Marysville Daily Herald*, 25 April 1856 (col. page2, col. 23).
110 "Excitement in Hoopa." *Humboldt Times*, 13 April 1861.
111 Herbert M. Hart, Colonel. USMC (Retired). "Fort Baker" – Essay. Retrieved April 15, 2019; http:www.militarymuseum.org/FtBakerI.html

Olmstead, Hyrom Lyon, Stephen Adams and another unknown individual.

Back in Humboldt county about 2 miles from Elk Camp, while unaware, local natives attacked the house of a man named Neill Hill. At the time, the homeowner was not present. He did however have a friend, Mr. Miller over for personal matters. Local natives would end up wounding him in the melee, but he managed to escape to Elk Camp. Mr. Hill's house would end up being burned to the ground.[112] Shortly afterward while at work, Mr. Albee who was the postmaster at Albeeville was murdered by local natives. His post office was burned to the ground and the Bald Hill post office was razed as well.[113]

These frustration of the communities would have been felt around the whole northern California region. A further example here would be near Chico, California:

"The killing of the Lewis children by the Mill Creek Indians was in the Summer of 1863 on the fifth or sixth of July. Sam Lewis lived on Dry Creek, seventeen miles southeast of Chico on Cherokee road. His children were going to school about two miles from their home. The elder boy, Jimmy, eleven years old, the girl, Thankful, nine, and Little Johnny, six. The little fellow did not go to school regularly but on this particular day asked to go and his mother let him go. As they were returning home

---

112 "From Humboldt." *Alta California*, 14 August 1862.
113 "From Northern California." *Alta California*, 29 November 1862.

in the evening the little boy wanted a drink. They left the road and went to the creek and lay down to drink.

"The oldest boy was drinking, the little boy and sister were standing waiting for him. The first thing they knew they heard a shot and Jimmy was shot in the back and pitched forward in the water. Four Indians appeared and began throwing rocks and boulders on him to make sure he was dead. The little boy and girl stood looking on, trembling with fear. Six other Indians then joined them, one of them had one big foot and one small one. This was Big Foot, the Chief of the Mill Creeks. They then started for the hills.

"They forced the children along until way in the night, until they came to Nance Canyon, where they camped. The little girl held the little boy on her lap and did not sleep. They left camp before daylight. Johnny began to cry. He and the little girl were barefooted. When the little boy began to weaken four of the Indians took him back out of sight of the girl. She said, "You are going to kill little brother, let me go and kiss him." They said, "No, he is all right." She said she knew they had killed him when they came back, as Big Foot had the little boy's hat on his head and one had his clothes.

"They then crossed Butte Creek and then Little Chico Creek and between Little and Big Chico Creeks they rounded up some cattle and shot a steer of General Bidwell's. They skinned it and made moccasins, which they tied on their feet. They cut strips of meat and ate it raw, the blood running over their chins. They wanted the little girl to eat it, but she would not. They cut a lot of meat to take with them. They were heavily loaded. The girl had a pair of gold ear rings in her ears. Two Indians attempted to tear them out. She told them she would give the ear rings to them. They began to fight as they both wanted them. She stopped the fight by giving one to each of the Indians.

"The Indian who had her in charge was lame and when they crossed the Big Chico Creek he and the girl were some distance behind the others. She told him she wanted to rest and for him to go and get some of them to help him with his load of meat as they could not keep up. He said, "You can rest if you want, run, if you do, I shoot." She sat down behind a large boulder. The Indian went up the hill until he was out of sight.

"She then rolled down the hill until she came to the creek, she jumped in and ran down it until the water got too deep. She then ran up the bank and down the creek until she saw a drift pile and she crawled under it and lay very still. Soon she heard them talking as they were looking for her. Finally all was still. She crawled out and ran down the bank of the creek to the Thomasson home and was met at the door by Mrs. Thomasson, in whose outstretched arms she fell.

"She told them how the Indians had had her and she got away. Mrs. Thomasson gave her dinner and washed her feet and greased them and made her as comfortable as possible. Just then, Nath. Thomasson came on horseback. He asked if she could go back the way the Indians came. She said she could, so Mrs. Thomasson put a pillow on the horse behind the saddle and put her on it. They went to the butchered steer and when they got to Little Chico Creek the horse could not get up the bluff, so he took the road and took her home. When they got there Mr. Lewis and his neighbors had found the elder boy and had just buried him.

"In the meantime when the children did not come home Mr. Lewis thought they had stayed with their grandmother, who lived near the schoolhouse but he could not rest. The next morning he saddled his horse and went to see where they were and as he was passing Mr. Ackley's house, Ackley said, "Where are you going, Sam?" He said that he was going to see why the children did not come home. Mr. Ackley said. "They passed here before sundown."

"Mr. Lewis said, "My children are killed by the Indians." He then rode back and saw the Indian's tracks in the road and rode home and told Mrs. Lewis. He then notified his neighbors and they soon found Jimmy, the murdered boy.

"When Mr. Thomasson came with the little girl she said she could take them to the place where she last saw Johnny. So she directed them and when they got to the place she told them to hunt for him. They soon found him where he had been thrown in a large manzanita bush. He had been beaten with clubs and rocks and stripped naked. He was so bruised and beaten they could not dress him to bury him. They wrapped him in a sheet and laid him in the coffin. In the morning when they left the camp in Nance Canyon one of the Indians left the others and went to the valley. The little girl did not know if he went to the Neal Rancheria or to the Bidwell Rancheria.

"This brutal murder aroused the whole country, so there was a mass meeting held at the Pentz Ranch about two miles from the Lewis home. People came from all over the county, about five hundred in number. Some wanted to kill all the Indians in the valley and in the hills. General Bidwell was there and plead for his Indians, saying he knew them to be innocent, and I believe they were.

"All the Indians in the hills were notified to be at the Bidwell Rancheria by a certain date or if caught in the hills after that date they would be shot on sight. A great many came and one day was set for Mr. Lewis and the little girl to come and investigate. They took the little girl and led her by the row of Indians. She finally stopped and took a good look at one of the Indians and said: "He looks just like the one that left the others the morning they killed Johnny."

"There was another Indian who had the name of being a bad one. It did not take more than suspicion to shoot an Indian in those days. They quickly tied their hands behind them and took them just to the outskirts of the town and there Mr. Lewis and six or seven of his neighbors tied the Indians to two small trees and Mr. Lewis and the others all shot at once and two Indians went to the Happy Hunting Ground."[114]

---

114 Moak, S. (1923). *The Last of the Mill Creeks and Early Life in Northern California*. Retrieved from http://www.loc.gov/resource/calbk.173

A BOIL OVER

These conflicts would happen to culminate and boil over. All over northern California, revenge and retaliation became common place between the settlers and the local native tribes. Even the United States Government, through their best attempts to control, minimize and subdue at all levels, any attempts at domestic unrest between the two parties. Requests all over the state of California from town governments for federal assistance went overlooked at times, and usually put on the lowest levels of legislative priority. It was due to the cataclysmic explosion of conflict in the prior decade that the citizens of Humboldt County would finally have enough of the hostile problems... and in their eyes... put an end to the issues.

In the fall of 1858, a rancher by the name of Paul Boynton, was working at his ranch located ten miles east of Union (Arcata). He was immediately shot dead by local natives. Austin Wiley, the editor for the Humboldt Times, mentioned earlier in the week that four Humboldt settlers were murdered, and four wounded by local native tribesmen. Later that month the U.S. Army sent a representative to take a look at the areas between Mad River and Redwood Creek. There, they would examine the state of hostilities and report a finding to the commander of the U.S. Army's Pacific Division.

Upon inspection of the area between Mad River and Redwood Creek, State Adjutant General W. C. Kibbe reported 300 to 350 "warriors," and even further he stated:

"The hostile tribe was generally well armed with rifles... The warfare they were waging did not seem to be entirely a predatory one. The Indians cared little for plunder, and were seeking to destroy men and animals, but would shoot a man or Indian for his gun, being anxious to obtain arms. They also sent the friendly Indians with gold dust to the camp to purchase guns and ammunition for them, and frequently offered $150 for a rifle worth only $10.15."

Cattle ranch owner James C. Ellison would end up killed after chasing down some local natives from the Nongatis tribe, attempting to hold them accountable for depredations against his stock of cattle. Mr. Ellison was a respected man of the settler community. The American communities of northern California saw these hostile incursions by the local natives as an act of war by foreign combatants. A public town-hall meeting was held by E. L. Davis, who was a former state assemblyman and made Humboldt County his home. In holding to the Second Amendment of the U.S. Constitution, a militia unit was formed at the meeting to protect life and property – any

American Citizens Constitutional right.¹¹⁵ They were called the Humboldt Volunteers, who were said to be funded by sympathetic Hydesville residents.¹¹⁶

The following letter was received by Governor Weller from the citizens of Union (Arcata):

"It has now been two months since the Indians in this vicinity started in open hostility to us, though so far they have confined their operations to the trail connecting this County to Weaverville. This being our direct channel of communication with the Sacramento Valley, and a trail over which the United States Mail must pass once a week, it is of the utmost importance that it should be kept open. The Indians on this trail first manifested their hostility to us by shooting a man who was traveling alone. We supposed that a few men would be sufficient to punish the Indians and make them ask for peace, and accordingly, a party was organized, provided for by private means and sent in search of the hostiles. "

"After trailing the Indians for several days, they were attacked from ambush and one man was killed. In the meantime their camp which they had left unguarded was attacked, and ten mules were killed. This party consisted

---

115 Hamilton, Alexander, James Madison, and John Jay. "Constitution of the United States." In *The Federalist Papers*, 5th ed., p. 182. New York: Washington Square Press, 1972. **Also see: U.S. Constitution, Section 8, Clause (2),(9),(14),(15) – in legitimate explanation to the legal actions taken by both settlers and U.S. government.
116 A notice of this meeting is attached to the militia company's organization sheets, Adjutant-General's Office. *Sacramento Union, March 2, 1860, page 2, column 2.

of only twelve men. Subsequently, another party of twenty-five men went out who were provisioned at a heavy private expense. In endeavoring to drive the Indians from the vicinity of the trails, they were fired upon in a deep canyon, and one man was killed, another wounded. The company has now disbanded, not feeling inclined to incur further danger and hardships at their own expense."

"The trails are now closed, there being no travel over them except by night or in large parties. The question now is what is- there to.be done? There are no troops here at the garrison and the people are not able to carry on a war at their own expense. The people of the county are of the opinion that if the militia could be called out, and arms furnished, the merchants would feel encouraged to furnish supplies, and wait for the State to pay. We can furnish the men if they can only be supplied."[117]

It was in February that a group of individuals of prominence, as well as members of the Humboldt Volunteers, would swear an oath of secrecy to deter the native depredations once and for all. And, with over ten years of constant native thefts and murders – the pot finally boiled over. In the early hours of February 26th 1860, The unknown members of the volunteer militia unit took to the Humboldt County, and began to systematically attack and destroy twelve local native village sites in a span of a week.

---

[117] Letter from A. Wiley to Governor Weller, State Archives, CA State Capitol.

They also occurred on the lower Eel River, the South Spit at Table Bluff in Fortuna, Humboldt Point (Rio Dell), Elk River, Eagle Prairie (Rio Dell) and Bucksport (just under Fort Humboldt). Dulawat village on Indian Island – just across the bay – was by far the most ruthless, brutal and savage of the attacks. Native men, women and children were killed off in the most barbaric ways, leaving few survivors. There was no mercy to be given. An absolute human failure in who the attacks were carried out against. This also proved and pushed the necessity of the U.S. government in northern California at the time, mostly as a temporary police force in northern California.

Mr. Davis, the lead facilitator of the Humboldt Volunteers would send a letter to the California State Governor:

"This company is needed for the protection of lives & property & if we do not get it we will never ask the state again & I for one shall oppose paying any more state Taxes & [we will] fight our own battles in our own way—Exterminate the Indians from the face of the earth as far as this county is concerned. In fact, the little mess at Indian Island near Eureka is only a beginning if we can't get our just protection from [the] state or [federal] government that American citizens are entitled to."[118]

---

[118] E. L. Davis, letter to Governor Downey, April 3, 1860, Indian War Papers, folder F3753:567.

CONCLUSION

In 1864, government commissioners were selected to find reservations for both the Modoc and Klamath tribes. In October of that year a treaty was signed in agreement by both parties. It was in 1865 more natives would be gathered to the specified reservations. By 1867 "...the country becoming settled up, and conflicts constantly arising between settlers and Indians, it was deemed best to permanently locate the Indians... They stayed contently, receiving their portion of the beef and flour provided until April 1869, when a portion of them... under the leadership of Captain Jack..." Captain Jack was the Klamath tribe Chief. "...taking some fancied offense at the action of the Klamath's decamped from the reservation..."[119] In this example, the Klamath tribe in 1869, made the choice to leave their reservation, even after signing and having the treaty ratified. This would again, cause commotions and depredations among the natives and settlers.

---

119 "An Account of the Modocs." *The Yreka Union*, 8 February 1873, col. page 1, col.6.-7.

The two parties would continue to have violent conflicts for some time. The local tribes would be relocated by the U.S. government for their own physical protections. This also enabled the U.S. government to maintain control and security over the newly formed state, as this was a continually hostile domestic situation. A report was made on the condition of affairs in native territory and California. In this document, the U.S. government further stated their true feelings and intentions behind the legalities of conflict between native tribes and settlers. At this period in time, all other U.S. domestic policies concerning native tribes and settlers had essentially failed outright. The civil unrest was too much political weight to handle.

Professor C.C. Painter, and agent of the Indian Rights Association would write:

"The theory under which the law should be interpreted and administered is this: The law contemplates the best interest of the Indian, and was intended to protect that interest, rather than to give extraordinary advantages to a white trader for enriching himself. The whole management of Indians has been abnormal, with little or absolutely no opportunity for the natural laws regulating social life to operate. Everything is controlled by arbitrary laws and regulations, and not by moral, social, or economic principles.

"Common sense, educated by long experience, has taught us, long since, that the natural laws of demand and supply will meet the wants of a community more wisely and economically than can be done under the most careful arbitrary regulations. No commissary department, however wise and able, could supply the daily needs of a great city like New York or Philadelphia as cheaply, safely, regularly, and with so little friction as does this simple law of demand and supply left free to operate upon the myriad agencies which, all over the world, are freely cooperating to this end. The sooner it is settled that the Indian belongs to the human family, that his needs must be met in the same way and under the same economic laws as in the case of all other human beings, the better it will be for him and for us who are so much perplexed with the difficulties of our problem— difficulties we foolishly create and then by most stupid methods undertake to solve."[120]

As far as being out west was concerned; it was a pricey issue to deal with. Especially for the U.S. government, and the statistics are evidence enough. Between the years 1849 to 1885, there were 3,846 native depredation claims filed with the U.S. Department of Interior. This cost the federal government nearly $14,000,000 dollars in losses.[121] Today, that would be worth upwards of $451,612,903.[122]

---

120 "The Condition of Affairs in Indian Territory and California. A Report." The Library of Congress. Accessed April 20, 2019. http://www.loc.gov/resource/calbk.052.
121 "Depredation Claims and Liabilities of the United States to Indians." Access Genealogy. Last modified September 29, 2014. https://www.accessgenealogy.com/native/depredation-claims-and-liabilities-of-the-united-states-to-indians.htm.
122 "Inflation Calculator." DaveManuel.com. Accessed May 9, 2019. https://davemanuel.com/inflation-calculator.php.

1845-1870 An Untold Story of Northern California

The many Indian hostilities that occurred against the settlers of Northern California were represented in many private newspapers.[123] One citizen wrote, "...the Indians had been in the habit of killing cattle, which had led to the killing of some Indians, after which the Indians availed themselves of every opportunity to kill whites."[124]

Again we face two solid facts. First, the humble truth is Native Americans did target civilians for theft and murder; secondly, there was absolutely no pre-existent consensus among whites that all Native Americans deserved such treatment or ill-conduct. Such an example speaks from an article from the Sacramento Union, written to the editor by early California settlers. They mentioned their feelings given due to Indian displacement by settlers. They saw it truly as the responsibility of the U.S. government to assist in a completely peaceful transition for the indigenous because of the endless killing, a full transition did become necessary.[125]

---

123 "Indian-white Relationships in Northern California, 1849-1920, in the Congressional Set of United States Public Documents." WorldCat.org. Accessed May 21, 2019. https://www.worldcat.org/title/indian-white-relationships-in-northern-california-1849-1920-in-the-congressional-set-of-united-states-public-documents/oclc/24555343.

124 CUTRER, THOMAS W. "WE ARE MEN AND BRAVES: INDIAN WARFARE IN THE FAR WEST." In *Theater of a Separate War: The Civil War West of the Mississippi River, 1861–1865*, 116-32. Chapel Hill: University of North Carolina Press, 2017. http://www.jstor.org.ezproxy.snhu.edu/stable/10.5149/9781469631578_cutrer.12.

125 *The Beacon*. "The Digger Indian Reservations, and C." December 15, 1858, pp. 1, col 6., article 1., vol. 2, no. 39.

Daniel L. Smith

In late May of 1863, messengers from the Klamath tribes contacted Colonel Olney at Fort Gaston requesting a permanent peace. Of course, only provided that the tribe be forgiven all of their depredations against the California settlers and the U.S. Army. As a subtle admission of guilt, the Colonel was having second thoughts of accepting this offer of peace "... and should not even listen to them."[126] Such forgiveness seemed inappropriate considering so many settler's lives were taken. In a court of law in the United States, when an offender to a crime knows they would be found guilty by judge and jury, they typically opt to defer settlement out of court. Usually to avoid further consequences.

The complex issues regarding the American settling of Northern California's landscape will always be a factor in our history that will forever be discussed and argued over. The issues of indigenous hostilities of Northern California would continue sporadically into the late-1800s. In the end, all other U.S. domestic policies concerning native tribes and settlers had essentially failed. The state and federal governments would ultimately move to permanently fix all local tribes onto federal reservations. American settler's to Northern California would soon feel the relief from war, and freedom from local native depredations. This may not have manifested into the peaceful transition that some were hoping for, however,

---

126 "A Voice From Hoopa." *Humboldt Times, 23 May 1863.*

regardless of personal theory and opinion; fact is absolutely fact.

In general it was a turbulent time of lawlessness, vice, and very little government presence. For settlers, it was a test of pro-activeness, personal determination, and faith. For local natives, it was a test of cultural resilience and in certain times survival, in an era of complete tribal decline. Humans since the beginning of civilization have continually looked for justice and retribution whenever they had been perceived as being wronged morally and/or ethically. A pastor once stated "Civilization around the globe has allowed for a grand total of 4 years of genuine peace since the beginning of time. This means, that at any one time, humanity is warring against one another."[127]

There is only one way an event can play out, and in life there are only four points-of-view:

The aggressors, the victims, the speculators, and God's.

---

[127] Ingram, Chip. "Sermon - C.S.N. Radio 93.7FM." Lecture, Living On The Edge Radio, Venture Christian Church, San Jose, CA., August 2019.

Bibliography

"A Judicial Farce." Lassen Advocate, 12 August 1897, page 2, col. 1. (vol. 31, no. 47.)

"A Voice From Hoopa." Humboldt Times, 23 May 1863.

Aaron Fichtelberg, "Chapter 3 - International Criminal Justice." In Crime Without Borders: An Introduction to International Criminal Justice, p. 33. Upper Saddle River: Prentice Hall, 2008.

Alexander Hamilton, John Jay, and James Madison. "Constitution of the United States." In The Federalist Papers. New York: Pocket Books, 1964.**Also see: U.S. Constitution, Section 8, Clause (2),(9),(14),(15) – in legal explanation to the pro-active actions taken by both settlers and U.S. government.

Albert Hurtado, Indian Survival on the California Frontier (New Haven and London: Yale University Press, 1988).

"Hardly a Farm House--A Kitchen without Them": Indian and White Households on the California Borderland Frontier in 1860." The Western Historical Quarterly13, no. 3 (1982): p. 256. doi:10.2307/969413.

"An Account of the Modocs." The Yreka Union, 8 February 1873, col. page 1, col.6.-7.

Anthony J. Bledsoe, Indian Wars of the Northwest: A California Sketch. San Francisco : Bacon & Company, 1885.

1845-1870 An Untold Story of Northern California

Anthony Delano, 1854. Life on the Plains and among the Diggings. Auburn, NY: Miller, Orton & Mulligan. Reprint, Alexandria, VA: Time-Life Books, 1981.

"Appropriations for 1856 for Support of the Government." Marysville Daily Herald, 25 April 1856 (col. page2, col. 23).

Bodie Hodge, and Roger Patterson. "Animism (Spiritism)." In World Religions & Cults Volume 2: Moralistic, Mythical and Mysticism Religions, pp. 230. Green Forest : New Leaf Publishing Group, 2016.

"California Militia and Expeditions Against the Indians, 1850 - 1859." The California State Military Museum. Accessed April 25, 2019. http://militarymuseum.org/MilitiaandIndians.html.

Charles L Camp, and George C. Yount. "The Chronicles of George C. Yount: California Pioneer of 1826." California Historical Society Quarterly 2, no. 1 (1923): 3-66. http://www.jstor.org.ezproxy.snhu.edu/stable/25177691

Charles A. Murdock. A Backward Glance at Eighty, Recollections & Comments,. San Francisco, California: Paul Elder & Co., 1921. http://www.loc.gov/resource/calbk.137.

Chip Ingram. "Sermon - C.S.N. Radio 93.7FM." Lecture, Living On The Edge Radio, Venture Christian Church, San Jose, CA., August 2019.

"Citizens of Crescent City." The California State Military Museum: Last modified August 10, 2017. http://militarymuseum.org/CrescentCity.html.

Daily National Democrat. "Portland Maine Transcript." October 26, 1858, pp. 2, col 1. Vol. 1, no. 63.

Daily National Democrat. "Untitled." August 19, 1858, pp. 2, col 3., vol. 1, no. 7.

Daniel L. Smith

Daniel L. Smith, Our America: Our Life & Our Culture. Eureka, CA.: Independent, 2018. Print.

David Lester, Crime and the Native American. eBook Collection (EBSCOhost) Printed: 2/25/2019

Daily National Democrat. "Portland Maine Transcript." October 26, 1858, col 1. Vol. 1, no. 63.

Daily National Democrat. "Untitled." August 19, 1858, pp. 2, col 3., vol. 1, no. 7.

Dame Shirley, California in 1851[-1852] ; the letters of Dame Shirley, (San Francisco: The Grabhorn Press, 1933).

"Depredation Claims and Liabilities of the United States to Indians." Access Genealogy. Last modified September 29, 2014. https://www.accessgenealogy.com/native/depredation-claims-and-liabilities-of-the-united-states-to-indians.htm.

Donald Lutz. "The Relative Influence of European Writers on Late 18th Century American Political Thought," American Political Science Review, LXXXVIII (1984).

David J. Weber. The Spanish Frontier in North America (New Haven: Yale University Press, 1992).

E. L. Davis, letter to Governor Downey. April 3, 1860, Indian War Papers, folder F3753:567.

"Excitement in Hoopa." Humboldt Times, 13 April 1861.

Freeman M. Tovell, At the Far Reaches of Empire: The Life of Juan Francisco De La Bodega Y Quadra. University of British Columbia Press, 2008. ISBN 978-0-7748-1367-9.

"From Humboldt." Alta California, 14 August 1862.

"From Northern California." Alta California, 29 November 1862.

"From the North." Marysville Daily Herald, 18 November 1855. col. page 2, col. 3.

1845-1870 An Untold Story of Northern California

"From Yreka." Shasta Courier, 16 June 1855, col. page 2, col. 2.

George Gibbs' Journal, Astoria, Oregon, Oregon Territory, 1850-1853, Smithsonian Archives, Capital Gallery Building, Washington D.C. "5, 6, 7." (note: journal pages were unnumbered.)

Geyle Olson-Raymer, "The Discovery, Exploration, and Founding of Spanish California." HSU – Dept. of History. Last modified Dec. 31, 2014. http://users.humboldt.edu/ogayle/hist383/Discovery.html. Print.

Gordon C. Roadarmel, "Some California Dates of 1861." California Historical Society Quarterly 39, no. 4. p. 357. (1960): 289-308. doi:10.2307/25155350.

Handbook of American Indians, north of Mexico (Bureau of American ethnology, Bulletin no. 30, edited by Fredrick M. Hodge – Washington, 1907-1910).

Herbert M. Hart, Colonel. USMC (Retired). "Fort Baker" – Essay. Retrieved April 15, 2019; http:www.militarymuseum.org/FtBakerI.html

Herbert Ziegler and Jerry Bentley. Bentley, Traditions & Encounters: A Global Perspective on the Past, 6th ed. New York, NY: McGraw-Hill, 2014.

Hubert H. Bancroft, Native Races (San Francisco, 1883), vols. 1, 3, 4.

"How the Indians Get Their Lead." Marysville Daily Herald. 21 November 1855, col. page 2, col. 3.

"How Beer Gave Us Civilization." The New York Times. Last modified October 19, 2018. http://www.nytimes.com/2013/03/17/opinion/sunday/how-beer-gave-us-civilization.html?_r=0.

Hinton R Helper,. "The Land of Gold. Reality Versus Fiction." The Library of Congress. Accessed April 22, 2019. http://www.loc.gov/resource/calbk.075.

"Humboldt Volunteers." The California State Military Museum. Accessed April 12, 2019. http://www.militarymuseum.org/HumboldtVolunteers.html.

"Humboldt News." Alta California, 15 October 1862.

"Humboldt News." Alta California, 17 August 1863. "Inflation Calculator." DaveManuel.com. Accessed May 9, 2019. https://davemanuel.com/inflation-calculator.php.

"Indians as Healers." Oroville Register, 21 July 1887, col. 1, col. 2 & 3.(vol. 10, no. 44) "Indian Medicinal Ideas" &"The Indian Medicine Man" [Globe Democrat]

"Indian Justice." Quincy Union, 31 December 1804, col. 1 col 3. (vol. 3 no. 10)

"Indian-white Relationships in Northern California, 1849-1920, in the Congressional Set of United States Public Documents." WorldCat.org. Accessed May 21, 2019. https://www.worldcat.org/title/indian-white-relationships-in-northern-california-1849-1920-in-the-congressional-set-of-united-states-public-documents/oclc/24555343.

JR, vol. 6, p. 101; vol. 7, p. 21; Leon Pouliot, "Paul le Jeune:, DCB, Lucien Campeau, "Pierre Biard", Dictonary of Canadian Biography (hereafter DCB) Toronto: University of Toronto Press, 1966-1994), vol. 1 & 3.

Kathy Sedler, "History of Humboldt County, California." Historic Record Co., Los Angeles, 1915.

L.A. Ackerman, Family instability and juvenile delinquency among Nez Perce's. American Anthropologist, 1971, 73, 595-603.

1845-1870 An Untold Story of Northern California

"Later From Humboldt." Alta California, 7 August 1862.

Letter from A. Wiley to Governor Weller, State Archives, CA State Capitol.

Levy, J. E., & Kunitz, S. J. "Indian Drinking." New York: Wiley, 1974.

"Indian Reservations, anomie, and social pathologies." Southwestern Journal of Anthropology, 1971, 27, 97-128.

Ltrs., Pacific Division, Record Group 393, National Archives Building. National Archives Microcopy. Wool to Thomas, Aug. 14, 1855; Townsend to Judah, Aug 30, 1855.; Jones to Buchanan, Oct. 18, 1855, RG393, NA.

M. A. Beliles, & S. K. McDowell, (2010). The Christian Form of Our Government. In America's Providential History (3rd ed., p. 186). The Providence Foundation.

Mary-Jo Wainwright, 1996. "Milestones in California History: The 1846 Bear Flag Revolt: Early Cultural Conflict in California." California History 75 (2): 25177573-25177573. Accessed 5 8, 2019. http://ch.ucpress.edu/content/75/2/25177573.

Matthew L.M. Fletcher, American Indian Tribal Law. N.p.: Aspen Publishing, 2011.

Michael Harrison, "Indian Problem Today." Paper, Sonoma State College. 1966.

M. P. Guéno, Native Americans, Law, and Religion in America. Oxford Research Encyclopedia of Religion, 2017. doi:10.1093/acrefore/9780199340378.013.140.

"Minority Report of the Special Joint Committee on the Mendocino War," in Appendix to Journals of the Senate, of the Eleventh Session of the Legislature of the State of California, (Sacramento: C.T. Botts, State Printer, 1860), 10.

"More About the Indian Difficulties in the North – Heroic Conduct of a Woman." Marysville Herald, 27 October 1855. col. 3 col 1).

"More Cause." Red Bluff Beacon, 29 June 1859. 2/1.

"More Indian Difficulties on the Klamath." Marysville Herald, 25 October 1855, col. 3 col. 1

"Native Americans Were Not Introduced to Alcohol by Europeans." Today I Found Out. Last modified November 17, 2013. http://www.todayifoundout.com/index.php/2013/11/native-americans-introduced-alcohol-europeans/.

Original California State Archives. California State Capitol. Photostatic copy's on file Adjutant General's Office (1856). A notice of this meeting is attached to the militia company's organization sheets, Adjutant-General's Office. *Sacramento Union, March 2, 1860, page 2, column 2.

Pamela Preston, "Native Americans and Substance Abuse." In Encyclopedia of Race and Crime, edited by Helen T. Greene and Shaun L. Gabbidon, 590-592. Thousand Oaks, CA: SAGE Publications, Inc., 2009. doi: 10.4135/9781412971928.n237

Philip M. Steyne, Gods of Power: A Study in the Beliefs and Practices of Animists (Columbia, SC: Impact International Foundation, 2011).

Robert A Carp, and Ronald Stidham. Judicial Process in America, 9th ed. Washington, DC: SAGE, 2001.

Robt. F. Heizer, Alan J. Almquist, The Other Californians, Prejudice and Discrimination under Spain, Mexico, and the U.S. to 1920 (Berkeley: University of California Press), 23.

1845-1870 An Untold Story of Northern California

Robt. F. Heizer, Alan J. Almquist, The Other Californians, Prejudice and Discrimination under Spain, Mexico, and the U.S. to 1920(Berkeley: University of California Press), 23.

Ronald Walters, American Reformers, 1815-1860. (Hill and Wayne, NY. Revised Edition)

Russel M. Posner, "A British Consular Agent in California: The Reports of James A. Forbes. 1843-1846." Southern California Quarterly, Vol. 53, No. 2 (UCP: JUNE 1971), p. 110. Accessed March 29th 2019. https://www.jstor.org/stable/41170342

Sacramento Union, October 30, 1855, page 2, column 2

Sacramento Union, January 19, 1855, page 2, column 1

S. Moak, The Last of the Mill Creeks and Early Life in Northern California. 1923. Retrieved from http://www.loc.gov/resource/calbk.173

The Beacon. "The Digger Indian Reservations, and C." December 15, 1858, pp. 1, col 6., article 1., vol. 2, no. 39.

"The Gold Rush Diary of George Bonniwell - August/September, 1850." Emigrant Road - Friday Aug 9 and 120 days out. Accessed April 20, 2019. https://www.emigrantroad.com/gold05.html.

Theodore Henry Hittell, (1898). History of California; Vol. 3, Book X, Chap XII – Treatment of Indians (cont.) San Francisco, CA: J.N. Stone.

The Beacon. "The Digger Indian Reservations, and C." December 15, 1858, pp. 1, col 6., article 1., vol. 2, no. 39.

"The California Letters of Edward Hotchkiss," in California Historical Society Quarterly, XII (June, 1933).

"The Condition of Affairs in Indian Territory and California. A Report." The Library of Congress. Accessed April 20, 2019. http://www.loc.gov/resource/calbk.052.

"The Honey Lake Troubles – Another U.S. Fort Wanted." San Francisco Bulletin, 28 October 1857

"The Indians' Account of the Creation of Man." Lassen Advocate, 6 April 1872, col. 4 col. 2. (vol. 7, no. 39)

"The Indian War." Daily Evening Herald, 26 August 1853, col. page 2, col. 2.

"The Last of the Mill Creeks, and Early Life in Northern California,." The Library of Congress. Accessed April 21, 2019. http://www.loc.gov/resource/calbk.173.

Thomas W. Cutrer, "WE ARE MEN AND BRAVES: INDIAN WARFARE IN THE FAR WEST." In Theater of a Separate War: The Civil War West of the Mississippi River, 1861–1865, 116-32. Chapel Hill: University of North Carolina Press, 2017. http://www.jstor.org.ezproxy.snhu.edu/stable/10.5149/9781469631578_cutrer.12.

Virginia P. Miller, "Yuki of Northern California." In Encyclopedia of Genocide and Crimes Against Humanity, edited by Dinah L. Shelton, 1177-1179. Vol. 3. Detroit, MI: Macmillan Reference USA, 2005. Global Issues in Context (accessed April 6, 2019). http://link.galegroup.com.ezproxy.snhu.edu/apps/doc/CX3434600372/GIC?u=nhc_main&sid=GIC&xid=410ccd53.

Walter R. Goldschmidt, and Harold E. Driver. "The Hupa: White Deerskin Dance." University of California Publications in American Archeology and Ethnology 35, no. 8 (1940).

William H. Ellison, "The Federal Indian Policy in California, 1846-1860." The Mississippi Valley Historical Review 9, no. 1 (1922), pp. 37-39. doi:10.2307/1886099.

"Indian Policy in California." 21, no. 1 (Fall), 2-3

"World's oldest brewery' found in cave in Israel, say researchers". BBC. Last modified September 15, 2018. https://www.bbc.com/news/world-middle-east-45534133.

www.ingramcontent.com/pod-product-compliance
Lightning Source LLC
Chambersburg PA
CBHW060836050426
42453CB00008B/716